D0167597

# Making Perfect Landings in Light Airplanes

# Making

# Perfect Landings
## IN LIGHT AIRPLANES

## Ron Fowler

**Blackwell**
Publishing

**THIS BOOK IS FOR** Helen

Illustrations by **Jan Avis**

Photographs by **John Tate**

Ron Fowler is the author of *Preflight Planning* (1983) and *Flying the Commercial Flight Test* (1988)

© 1984, 2000 Iowa State University Press

Blackwell Publishing Professional
2121 State Avenue
Ames, Iowa 50014

Orders:   1-800-862-6657
Office:    1-515-292-0140
Fax:       1-515-292-3348
Web site: www.blackwellprofessional.com

All rights reserved

Authorization to photocopy items for internal or personal use, or the internal or personal use of specific clients, is granted by Blackwell Publishing, provided that the base fee of $.10 per copy is paid directly to the Copyright Clearance Center, 222 Rosewood Drive, Danvers, MA 01923. For those organizations that have been granted a photocopy license by CCC, a separate system of payments has been arranged. The fee code for users of the Transactional Reporting Service is ISBN-13: 978-0-8138-1081-2/84 (hardcover); ISBN-13: 978-0-8138-0438-5/00 (paperback); ISBN-10: 0-8138-1081-7/84 (hardcover); 0-8138-0438-8/00 (paperback) $.10.

Printed on acid-free paper in the United States of America

First edition, 1984
First paperback edition, 2000

Library of Congress Cataloging in Publication Data

Fowler, Ron
    Making perfect landings in light airplanes.

    1. Airplanes—Landing. 2. Private flying. I. Title.
TL711.L3F69          1984          629.132′5213          83-22691
ISBN-13: 978-0-8138-1081-2 (hardcover); 978-0-8138-0438-8 (paperback)
ISBN-10: 0-8138-1081-7 (hardcover); 0-8138-0438-8 (paperback)

Last digit is the print number:  9  8  7  6  5

COVER PHOTOGRAPH: MOONEY AIRCRAFT CORPORATION

# CONTENTS

# INTRODUCTION

NO MATTER HOW LONG you have been a pilot and no matter what degree of skill you have attained, if you are to land perfectly you must exert a 100 percent effort toward that task. Many pilots resign themselves to imperfect landings merely because they are unaware of the simple fact that *even the pros must work at each landing.* Many pilots feel that sooner or later good landings are supposed to happen automatically. When this does not happen to them, they often feel they simply do not possess the mystical "flyer's instinct" that makes flying effortless. These pilots are then apt to accept imperfection as their lot, and their efforts are very likely to run at half throttle. But after discovering that even old pelicans must concentrate intensely to make seemingly effortless landings, they become quite willing to exert the needed effort.

This effort, however, is not only one of applying pilot skill during the landing itself but also one of acquiring knowledge long before the landing is at hand. Each landing situation (soft-field, strong crosswind, runway slope, etc.) presents its own complications, of which pilots must be aware and with which they must contend. In planning landings, pilots must know the true nature of the complications that are present and how they can be competently met with the degree of skill brought to the cockpit. And, too, pilots must know how to determine the airplane's ability to handle factors present in the landing situation.

A perfect landing therefore includes recognition of the landing situation and understanding of its true nature, knowledge of how to meet and weigh each required task against personal skill and limitation, and ability to evaluate the airplane's capacity to meet each challenge. These three skills are the only ones needed to produce that mystical "flyer's instinct."

The purpose of this book is to show how pilots can develop a keen sense of awareness in each of these three areas, and how to convert that awareness into perfect landings. Each chapter presents and defines a specific landing situation, so that pilots can quickly recognize it in the cockpit and plan procedures accordingly. The short-field landing, for example, presents several problems other than a runway of minimal length. Pilots, however, must quickly see through the guises, and put the short-field procedure into play. They must know the true nature of the factors they are up against before pilot procedures can be effective. In facing the short-field situation, for instance, pilots must know that in recent years the short field has accounted for more than a fair-average share of accidents for two simple reasons. But awareness must extend beyond knowing *what* factors must be faced. To effectively neutralize these, pilots must also know *why* they adversely affect landings, and *how* procedures will negate them. The chapters detail knowledge for every situation in specifics that can be used in any landing. There is very little theory here; it is mostly "nuts and bolts" practical application.

Each chapter will also teach you how to evaluate your present skill and your airplane's capability in many landing situations.

Often, a critical landing pushes both pilot and plane to the very limits of their abilities. In these tight situations, it is imperative that pilot procedures include fail-safe mechanisms that stop the action when the point of no return approaches; mechanisms that assure the pilot a safe out. The procedures herein do just that. The pilot flying that short-field approach, for example, uses three references that ensure safety even to those with mediocre skill and marginal aircraft.

Professional pilots do not think of a landing as one continuous maneuver. Instead, they think of it in terms of steps that provide intermediate goals; each step is completed before the next begins. This step-by-step method produces a seemingly effortless landing, because each individual step is easier than making the landing in one continuous move. Line drawings, designed to help you break down the landing into simple, logical steps are included. Photographs provide a pilot's-eye view of the visual clues that help you monitor the quality of each step in your landing. Understanding and using these visual references will produce perfection — or near perfection — landing after landing.

A condensed review following each chapter provides an in-the-cockpit reminder of procedures for use in facing critical landing situations.

This book, then, is one of awareness — a book to help you realize a *total awareness* of the situation facing you, of your plane, and of yourself in one phase of flight, that of landing an airplane.

While certainly within the grasp of the average pilot, attainment of this goal is no easy task. For in doing so, you must exert an effort to raise your own awareness level far above that of the average pilot. This effort goes well beyond that of reading the text; it is one of applied reason. As you read the described procedures, think back to past landing situations you have faced. Reason, in retrospect, how the outlined procedures would have helped. Then use that reasoning in similar landing situations you encounter in your hours aloft.

Is the ability to land perfectly worth the effort it takes to attain it? Yes, I feel that it is. *Perfect landing* can be defined as a noun and as a verb. But to the pilot descending behind a throttled engine, the term escapes the confinement of simple parts of speech and becomes an ideal for the flyer to seek. Perfect landings encapsulate three vital elements of the pilot's world — tradition, safety, and pride.

From the beginning of powered flight, pilots held the traditional role: masters of their airplanes, possessors of thorough knowledge of the art of flying, and skill above reproach. This level of competency is expected not only from fellow pilots but from the nonflying public as well. A passenger in a light aircraft expects and deserves a professional level of competency. All aviators, past and present, know that the landing is the most visible display of competency. An excellent landing ensures confidence. Anything less lessens the tradition.

A pilot's self-confidence holds the promise of safety. It is no coincidence that most aviation accidents happen during landing. The margin for allowable pilot error shrinks as we get closer and closer to the ground. It is primarily pilots whose landing approaches are filled with doubt and indecision, who "pull it back and hope for the best," that account for damaged airplanes and injured people.

Flying is one of the few remaining endeavors that allows us to command our own fate. Once in the air, pilots leave behind the battery of experts, knowing that they alone must analyze the task, weigh the risks, and command the decisions. Flying offers the pride of independence. Every pilot is entitled to share in that pride each time total awareness and 100 percent effort are employed in the delivery of a perfect landing.

**per·fect land·ing**     1. *noun.* the conclusion of a flight in which the plane is brought down and to rest exactly in accordance with the pilot's wishes. 2. *verb.* to return the plane to Earth in such a manner that the pilot's total awareness of the landing situation and complete control of the aircraft is obvious.

Author's definition

# 1 | Basic Considerations of a Normal Landing

TRY NOT TO CONFINE your landing procedure to the bounds normally placed on the maneuver — from point of touchdown to end of landing roll. To do so encourages you to delay planning your landing until you find yourself on short final, and the result often comes as a rude surprise ending to the flight, not the pleasantly expected conclusion.

Know that a well-thought-out landing begins 10 minutes out and ends with the plane clear of the runway and safely shut down. And don't try to execute the entire landing procedure as one continuous maneuver. Plan it as 10 separate steps, each with its own objective:

1. Descending to the destination airport.
2. Entering the traffic pattern.
3. Flying the traffic pattern.
4. Descending to the runway.
5. Rounding out.
6. Touching down.
7. Rolling out.
8. Clearing the runway.
9. Taxiing to the ramp.
10. Shutting down.

## Descending to the Destination Airport

Make the descent from your en route altitude an integral part of your landing. Plan the descent so you don't waste a minute as you move your airplane into position for a perfect pattern entry. This makes the most efficient use of your machine, and the extent of your planning (the hallmark of an experienced pilot) is apparent to your passengers. And, of even greater value, the attention you gave to detail several miles out helps you "rev up" that 100 percent effort for the steps that follow.

Here is how to manage your descent. If you have no more than 5000 feet to lose before you reach the traffic pattern, begin your descent to the airport 10 minutes out. This translates into 15 miles for a 90-MPH Cessna 152, for example, or 30 miles for a

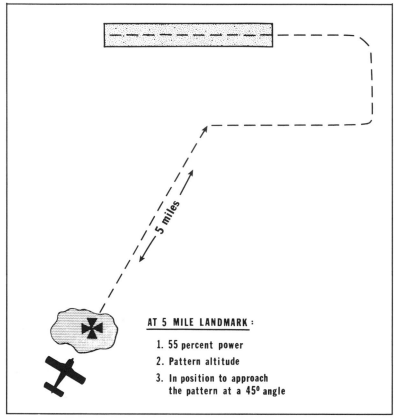

**AT 5 MILE LANDMARK :**

1. 55 percent power
2. Pattern altitude
3. In position to approach
   the pattern at a 45° angle

**Fig. 1.1.** Begin your approach to the pattern while still 5 miles out.

180-MPH Bonanza. Before you drop, figure the rate of descent that will put you at pattern altitude near your airport. If it is 3000 feet down to the pattern, for example, peg your VSI (vertical speed indicator) on 300 FPM for the 10-minute descent.

If you need to lose 6000 feet or more, begin your descent 20 minutes out, and estimate your rate of descent against that time. About 300 FPM for a 6000-foot descent, for example, or 500 FPM for 10,000 feet.

When you lower your airplane's nose to the desired rate of descent, reduce your power to prevent over-revving the engine or building up excessive speed. A maximum descent setting of 65 percent power works well in many light airplanes. This gives you a slight desirable increase in speed for an efficient letdown and protects the engine from rapid cooling. Remember, though, that the manifold pressure increases as you drop into denser air, so readjust the throttle (and mixture) every 2000 feet.

In most cases you will not aim your descent directly at the airport. Unless you are receiving radar vectors, plan to arrive at pattern altitude over a landmark 5 miles out — one that puts you in good position to approach the downwind leg at a 45-degree angle (Fig. 1.1). Determine the active runway early in your descent, either from radio communications or by wind direction from ground references. Then a quick look at the sectional chart lets you select a prominent landmark toward which to fly. This lengthy 45-degree approach at pattern altitude offers the best opportunity to spot traffic that is already in, approaching, or departing the pattern (Fig. 1.2). Your relatively low altitude frames the traffic against the skyline, rather than camouflaging it against the ground. Years ago, in case of engine failure, we

**Fig. 1.2.** A 45-degree approach to the traffic pattern offers a panoramic view of the entire airport traffic area. This approach allows you to pick up your traffic easily and to select landmarks that help visualize the pattern's ground track.

taught pilots to "keep 'em high" when approaching the airport. But today's engines are considerably more reliable, and the greater hazard now is a midair collision.

If you fly a high-performance retractable, give thought to your pattern speed as you cross your 5 mile landmark. Retractables decelerate slowly, so reduce power to 55 percent at 5 miles out. This gives your airplane a chance to slow to gear-extension speed as the downwind leg draws near.

Step one of your landing concludes with the airplane over a landmark 5 miles out, at pattern altitude, carrying 55 percent power, and in position to approach the downwind leg at a 45-degree entry.

## Entering the Traffic Pattern

If you fly a retractable-gear airplane, lower the wheels at one-half mile before turning downwind. This helps decelerate the streamlined airplane to flap-operating range as you enter the traffic pattern (Fig. 1.3).

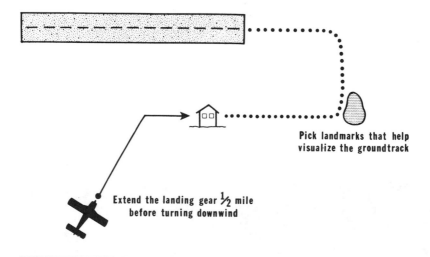

Pick landmarks that help visualize the groundtrack

Extend the landing gear ½ mile before turning downwind

**Fig. 1.3.** Enter the downwind leg at the midpoint of the runway at pattern altitude, slowing to pattern speed.

Just before you turn into the pattern, take a moment to pick up some landmarks that help you visualize the downwind leg's ground track. It is very difficult to maintain a straight track unless you visualize the path on the ground, particularly if you're dealing with a wind.

Plan on accomplishing 3 tasks as you complete your downwind turn (Fig. 1.4).

**Fig. 1.4.** Slow the plane to its pattern speed early on the downwind leg. Quickly establish a wind correction angle to maintain your visualized ground track. Execute your prelanding checklist.

1. Reduce throttle to slow the plane to 1.7 times stall (stall speed with flaps and gear up). About 2000 RPM or 20 inches works well for many small airplanes. You may want to experiment with slow flight to determine what works best for your airplane. This downwind speed allows time to organize a good traffic pattern yet is not so slow that it ties up traffic.
2. Based on the known wind, establish an estimated drift correction angle against your visualized ground track.
3. Exercise a simple prelanding checklist:
   a. Proper fuel tank; boost pump on.
   b. Gear indication "safe."
   c. Mixture and propeller set for possible go-around.
   d. Carburetor heat, if required.

Once you've established the downwind direction, quickly pick the three landmarks that assure accuracy and safety of your landing (Fig. 1.5):

1. Select a landmark to serve as a half-mile final-approach fix.
2. Pick a mark on the runway to use as your touchdown bulls-eye.
3. Select a point on the runway to serve as your go-around point.

A half-mile final-fix point offers several advantages to the pilot. The point offers, for example, an intermediate altitude

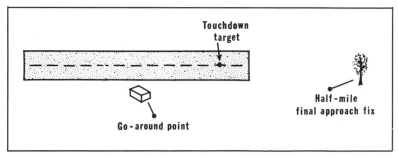

**Fig. 1.5.** While flying the downwind leg, select three landmarks that promote accuracy and safety.

objective in the descent from pattern altitude to touchdown. As we will see shortly, the pilot's objective is to place the plane 400 feet AGL (above ground level) over this point at approach speed. A half-mile final-fix point on every landing assures consistency. Pretty soon the pilot is an expert on that last half-mile of flying; it has been flown from the same altitude, at the same airspeed, landing after landing. The final-fix point is extremely valuable anytime a pilot needs to deviate from the normal pattern. If, for instance, the tower asks for an extended downwind or a 360 for spacing, the pilot with a final-fix landmark does not worry, knowing that no matter what happens to the *rest* of the pattern, this final half-mile is just like every other. The pilot also has the decided advantage of a visible landmark; it is a simple truth that we all fly better when we know our exact destination.

When landing at a paved airport, pick a particular center stripe as your touchdown target. If the airport is unusually busy and the runway long, pick your target to allow a quick exit to the taxiway. Under normal circumstances, however, the second centerline stripe from the numbers makes a good target. It is close enough to the runway's threshold to conserve landing distance, yet far enough up the runway to prevent a short landing. Pilots who try to "plant it on the numbers" run the risk of hitting short of the runway. Paved runways do not blend smoothly into the grass. They usually have a 6- to 8-inch lip. Catching this with your gear at touchdown speed seldom goes unnoticed.

Turf runways usually offer a ready-made target — the spot worn bare by the hometown pilots. Occasionally, at sod airports you can't find a significant mark on the runway itself, so select a marker alongside the runway to serve as a target. The point is however, have a visible touchdown target. For as we will soon see, we depend on the apparent movement of this mark to guarantee an accurate descent from our final-fix point.

Finally, pick a go-around point and decide downwind to make an immediate go-around if your tires haven't thumped by the time that point whizzes by. But don't put that decision off until things start going wrong and the airplane is skimming along an evaporating runway. Select a go-around point that gives a stop distance of at least 150 percent of the airplane's normal landing roll. This allows a safe margin in the event of an unforeseen stopping situation, such as defective brakes, a wet patch of runway, or an excessive touchdown speed.

You are finished with step 2 of your landing when you have visualized the pattern's ground track, reduced your power for pattern speed, performed your landing checks, estimated wind drift, and selected landmarks for your final fix, touchdown, and go-around.

## Flying the Traffic Pattern

Plan on a pattern speed of 1.7 times stall, but be ready and able to vary that airspeed somewhat. If there is a traffic jam ahead, for instance, slow-fly your entire pattern at approach speed. A pilot should experiment with nose pitch and engine power to learn the exact combination that holds the airplane's altitude at approach speed. The slow speed gives you extra reaction time in heavy traffic and prevents the need for an extended downwind.

If, on the other hand, you realize that a jam is developing behind you, don't hesitate to increase your downwind and base-leg speeds. Remember, though, to have your airplane slowed to approach speed as you reach your half-mile final-fix point — just extend the flaps further and reduce power.

Each pilot must decide when and how to apply flaps. Some pilots apply half the flaps they intend to use before turning base leg and the remaining half while on base — and this is sound. Other pilots apply a third of their intended flaps on downwind, a third on base, and a third on final — and this is sound too. The point is to have a definite procedure for lowering your flaps and use it consistently. You soon become expert at it.

For seemingly effortless landing, consider using partial flaps for normal landings, subject, of course, to the airplane's handbook recommendation. The pilot using partial flaps holds several advantages over pilots using either full flaps or no flaps.

An approach flown with partial flaps gives you greater flexibility than one flown with full flaps. If you are flying your approach with the flaps partially extended and suddenly need to extend your pattern, a slight squeeze of throttle works fine. The pilot with full flaps, on the other hand, needs a great wad of power to do the same job and ends up with a hard-to-manage airplane.

Say that two pilots are at the midpoint of their final legs — one flying with partial flaps, the other with full flaps — and they discover they are overshooting the landing. The pilot with partial flaps has only to extend the reserve flaps. The full-flap pilot has no reserve.

Partial flaps on the final leg are just as advantageous to pilots who decide they are undershooting. They need only a tad of throttle to extend the descent, and the airplane's pitch altitude remains virtually undisturbed. If you are an undershooting pilot with full flaps, however, you need to mash in considerable power to extend your descent. And the sudden disturbance of pitch and torque usually results in a landing that calls for an apology to your passengers.

An approach flown with partial flaps has an advantage over a no-flaps approach. Flaps add safety. They increase the margin between flying speed and stalling speed — if the pilot maintains the proper no-flaps approach speed throughout the application of flaps. Carrying partial flaps into the landing approach brings predictability to the descent, because, unless you know your airplane very well, you are apt to gain altitude when you extend that first notch of flaps. If you make your first flap application on short final to prevent an overshoot, you might find yourself ballooning even higher. No such altitude gain is likely to occur from lowering additional flaps, however, if partial flaps were carried into the approach.

Some pilots feel that they must not use flaps when landing in a crosswind. They think that flaps increase the plane's susceptibility to drift, but this is not the case. Flaps have very little to do with the airplane's tendency to drift in a crosswind landing. Ground speed is the true culprit. The slower the ground speed, the more the crosswind affects the plane. So go ahead and use flaps with the crosswind, but fly your approach at your airplane's proper no-flaps speed.

In normal landing, I usually land with half the flaps the wings offer and normally apply half this amount as I complete my downwind leg, lowering the rest on base leg. You must decide on your own procedure for using flaps, but do have a procedure and practice it.

Be mindful of wind in flying your traffic pattern. Carry a mental picture of its effect on each leg of the pattern. Use landmarks to help you visualize each leg and be able to pin down the drift with little difficulty. If you fail to visualize the desired ground track, you will probably drift.

If, on downwind you drift toward the runway, your resulting base leg will not allow time enough for your planned descent. If you find yourself in this position, you can easily compensate for the abbreviated base by extending your downwind to allow for a longer final leg. The pilot who allows the airplane to drift away from the runway on downwind risks an abnormally low approach. Again, you can easily compensate for this error by simply delaying the descent from pattern altitude.

If you anticipate a trailing wind on base leg, also expect a high ground speed on that leg. Compensate with a longer final, or widen your downwind to provide a lengthened base leg. Compensate for an expected head wind on base by either planning a shorter final leg or a shorter base leg. When you allow for the wind on base leg, the point is to anticipate the ground speed and plan both base and final so that the total time for the two legs remains normal (Fig. 1.6).

Allow for any trailing wind on base as you plan your turn to final. A base-leg tail wind can easily drift you right past your planned final leg. Then you are very apt to make too steep a turn at low speed and low altitude to quickly reestablish your intended ground track. A pilot can prevent any unwanted drift by simply turning from base to final a little early. If you find yourself swinging wide on your turn to final, you should plan to

**Fig. 1.6.** Whether you anticipate a headwind or a tailwind on base leg, anticipate the resulting ground speed. Then plan both base and final so that the total time for the two legs remains normal.

land further down the runway in order to make a shallow turn back to the desired final approach course. A head wind on base doesn't disturb a pilot's turn to final. The head wind tends to slow the action and gives the pilot extra time in which to plan the turn.

Anticipate any crosswind as you turn final. Then roll out a few degrees left or right of runway alignment to correct for the wind as you continue descending toward the touchdown.

Why is the traffic pattern square? Why not round? Or oval? Because the square pattern gives the pilot a series of clearing turns in a high-density area. And, equally important, perpendicular legs offer perpendicular movement between airplanes, which makes it easier for pilots to spot each other. So use the traffic pattern effectively. Search out traffic on the perpendicular leg ahead. When on downwind, look for traffic on both extended left and right base legs. After turning base leg, check the long final for arrivals. Once established on final, look quickly for airplanes using the other runways. Don't forget that someone may be using the opposite end of your runway. Search out the traffic, keeping two facts uppermost in your mind; most midairs happen during the landing phase of flight and studies show that the average pilot sees only a third of the significant traffic.

Think of flying your traffic pattern in terms of adjusting airspeed, managing the flaps, correcting for drift, and spotting traffic.

## Descending to the Runway

The landing descent begins at pattern altitude abeam the touchdown target and ends on short final with the airplane at the proper landing speed and an altitude that ensures a touchdown on the bull's-eye. The pilot's task in descending from pattern altitude to the runway is twofold: managing a constant approach airspeed and managing a consistent glide path (Fig. 1.7).

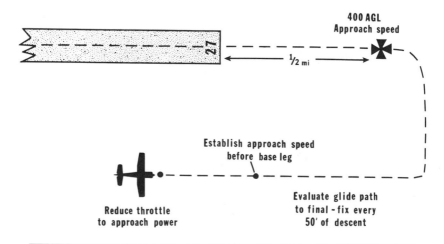

**Fig. 1.7.** Staying ahead of your plane during the descent to the runway is easy if you establish approach speed before turning base and evaluate your descent to the final-fix point.

The secret to a good approach lies in the pilot's ability to control airspeed. If the airspeed is constant throughout the approach, a consistent glide path is just a matter of making small power changes — a tad of additional power if the airplane starts to drop below the desired glide path or a smidge fewer RPMs if the airplane isn't descending steeply enough. It's as easy as moving the throttle. But if you let the airspeed stray, a smooth descent is extremely difficult, for you must simultaneously recapture the airspeed and maintain a smooth glide path throughout two changes in direction. Too many variables present an almost impossible task, like trying to hit a running jackrabbit with loose gun sights.

Slow to approach speed by further reducing throttle while on downwind as you draw abeam your touchdown target. Apply carburetor heat, if required. For the sake of a standardized procedure, pull the throttle to an arbitary setting suitable to your airplane. True, you probably will need to make minor changes in power to adjust for the wind, but *start* each descent with the same power setting. About 1700 RPM or 17 inches manifold pressure (MP) is reasonable for most small airplanes. With similar power settings, the entry to each approach becomes standard.

Practice this set procedure with each descent, and you soon become an expert on another element of landing — setting up the approach.

Remember that proper trim is the key to precise airspeed. Readjust trim with every change in power and each increment of flaps. Have your approach speed established before you turn base, and you gain two advantages. First, decelerating this early in the approach slows the action. You see the approach before you in slow motion, and you have no trouble staying ahead of your airplane. Second, you easily manage constant airspeed descent early in your approach.

Use the half-mile final-fix landmark to guarantee a smooth letdown from downwind to final. Start evaluating your glide path abeam your touchdown target, the moment you throttle back for the approach speed. The planned descent should place you, at approach speed, 400 feet AGL over the final-fix point (Fig. 1.8).

**Fig. 1.8.** Plan to cross your half-mile final-fix landmark 400 feet above the ground and at the correct approach speed.

Fly the descent smoothly, without radical power changes that may upset your airplane's pitch attitude.

You can accomplish this smooth descent by reevaluating your glide path every 50 feet. Simply know what you want the altimeter to read as you cross the final fix. Then as you complete your downwind and base legs, divide your attention between the altimeter and the landmark. A smooth descent then becomes a simple matter of monitoring "altitude to lose" versus "distance to fly." Make your response with small (less than 100 RPM or 1 inch MP) power changes each 50 feet, if needed; desperate bids with the throttle are unnecessary. You stand an excellent chance of gaining your half-mile final-fix point at exactly 400 feet AGL and maintaining approach speed with very nearly the same power setting with which you began the descent.

Professional pilots use this half-mile final fix to make their landings look easy. It gives them an intermediate goal in their

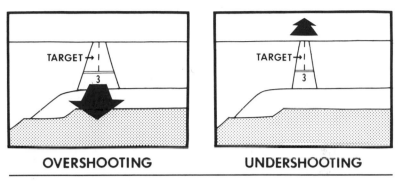

**OVERSHOOTING**            **UNDERSHOOTING**

**Fig. 1.9.** If you overshoot, the target appears to move downward and toward you. If the target moves upward and away, you are coming in too low.

descent to the runway, which guarantees an arrival on final that is neither dangerously low nor ridiculously high.

Once you are over your final fix, shift your attention to the next goal — the touchdown target. Use the apparent motion of the target to ensure an accurate letdown in the final half-mile of your approach. If the target appears to move upward or away from you, the glide path is too low, and you will land short of your mark (Fig. 1.9). Add a small amount of power to correct. If the target appears to move downward or toward you, the glide path is overshooting (Fig. 1.10). Reduce power slightly to achieve your

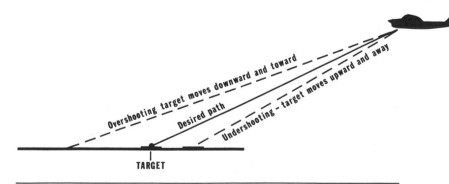

**Fig. 1.10.** The final approach path in profile shows why an incorrect descent makes the touchdown target appear to move.

target. Once the apparent movement of your touchdown spot stabilizes, your glide path is straight toward target. You actually touch down slightly beyond the target, since ground effect shallows the last moments of your glide. Hold the target motionless with a small throttle movements, and keep those power increments less than 100 RPM to prevent drastically altering your airplane's pitch attitude.

Consider the descent to runway complete as you approach the threshold with minimal power and a touchdown on target assured.

## Rounding Out

The round out brings the airplane from its approach speed and attitude to the touchdown speed and attitude. The pilot's main concerns during this brief segment of a landing are to smoothly withdraw the remaining power from the engine and to have the airplane's nose in the landing attitude as the tires touch. (Crosswind correction during the round out, touchdown, and roll-out segments is a subject in itself and is covered in detail in Chapter 2.)

Begin your round out by slightly lifting the nose from its approach attitude and reducing power slightly as the threshold draws near. Keep your hand on the throttle during the round out and coordinate your power reduction with change in pitch attitude, so that the throttle hits idle just as the tires touch. Carrying a small amount of power into the round out minimizes the prospect of "dropping it in" if you misjudge on the high side. A smooth and constant reduction to an idle-power touchdown helps prevent unnecessary floating. A few RPMs carried to touchdown also lets the engine respond to a possible last-second go-around.

Two visual references ensure a proper touchdown in today's nosewheel airplanes — the tip of the nose and the far end of the runway. Once over the threshold, note the apparent gap between the tip of your airplane's nose and the runway's far end. Then, with each few feet of descent to the touchdown, raise the nose

**Fig. 1.11.** For a perfect touchdown attitude in most light tricycle-gear airplanes, use a visual reference. Time the pitch attitude so that the nose covers the far end of the runway just as the tires touch.

inch by inch to close the gap between it and the runway's end. For a perfect landing attitude, time the pitch movement so the nose just covers the far edge of the runway as the tires touch (Fig. 1.11).

This reference — nose against the end of the runway — is an excellent aid in practicing landing procedures. It lets you evaluate your pitch control during each round out. If, for example, you still see runway as you land, you did not get your nose high enough soon enough. Or, if the nose hides the runway before you touch, you pitched your nose too high too soon. The reference gives you a visual goal for the touchdown attitude and makes the nosetip's progress toward that goal plain. (Note: Many pilots think they are looking at the airplane's nose but are in reality seeing the top edge of the instrument panel. That won't work for our purposes. The panel is very near the airplane's pitch-attitude pivot point, and it has little upward movement as you apply nose-up pitch. You need to see the nose — and that means stretching your neck to see over the panel.)

The round-out segment of a normal landing is a coordinated blend of reducing power and increasing pitch attitude. It concludes with the engine at zero thrust, the nose in its touchdown attitude, airspeed near stall, and the tires settling to the runway.

## Touching Down

A good touchdown begins with the airplane easing its main gear onto the runway and ends with the pilot gently lowering the nosewheel to the ground. The pilot's main job now, apart from handling the crosswind (covered in Chapter 2), is to prevent the abuse that gravity can inflict as a ton or so of airplane comes down on a chunk of concrete.

The pilot can best accomplish this with a good follow-through. When a modern light airplane touches down, a great deal of "stick travel" remains in the control column. A good follow-through uses this extra stick travel to ensure a super soft landing. The pilot must keep applying aft stick pressure as the tires touch. This prevents "stick freeze" in that moment before the tires touch, as the pilot anticipates the thump onto the runway. And the gear will hit with a hearty thump if you land with a motionless stick.

The pilot should use follow-through to keep the nosewheel away from the pavement as long as possible. A perfect follow-through brings the stick back to the stop just as the nosewheel touches the ground. This prevents the shock that a slammed nosegear sends to the airframe—particularly to delicate engine mounts.

If you *do* find yourself dropping the nosewheel hard against the runway, it is probably a holdover from your student training. It is a habit developed by pilots who learned landings by the touch-and-go method, where the nosegear gets slammed into place for the ensuing takeoff. It is a hard habit to break, but break it you must if you are to deliver smooth touchdowns.

## Rolling Out

The roll-out (those seconds from the time the nosewheel touches until you start braking for the exit) is a critical segment of the landing insofar as passenger confidence is concerned. The pilot's prime responsibility is directional control. A sudden swerve and a tire screech has made many a passenger go Greyhound for the return trip.

Perfect directional control during the roll-out requires 100 percent effort. You cannot use this time to retract flaps, close the carburetor heat, or switch a radio frequency but must keep eyes locked on the center stripes ahead, hand ready on the throttle, and toes nimble on the rudder bar. You must delay all other cockpit chores until you have cleared the runway and brought the airplane to a stop.

Remember that the airplane is subject to aileron drag or adverse yaw during the roll-out. That means that if you turn the control wheel in one direction, the airplane slews in the opposite direction. If you turn the wheel to the left, for example, the left aileron is raised and protected from the onrushing wind by the wing's curved upper surface. The right aileron, however, lowers beneath the wing and digs into the wind, and the airplane slews right.

## Clearing the Runway

Under normal circumstances, begin braking only after your airplane has coasted to fast taxi speed. If a critical situation requires a quick stop, however, go ahead and lean into those brakes during a fast landing roll. Just be sure not to lock the tires and do brake evenly to keep the airplane going straight astride the centerline. Fast stops add wear and tear to airplane, pilot, and passenger, but they are occasionally unavoidable.

When you exit the runway, taxi at least 100 feet down the taxiway before stopping. The pilot landing behind you may be inattentive and unaware of your position until swinging off the runway, so leave some "missing room."

For your passenger's comfort and peace of mind, avoid bringing the airplane to a lurching stop that reminds everyone they are wearing seat belts and shoulder harnesses. Brake the same way you do in a car. The instant before the airplane stops, ease off the brake pressure.

Be sure to come to a complete stop before you change frequency, retract flaps, close carburetor heat, or open windows. If you direct your eyes inside the cockpit while the airplane is moving, you risk bumping into something and raising your cost of flying to prohibitive.

## Taxiing to the Ramp

Keep one rule of thumb in mind anytime you taxi an airplane: *Other pilots probably are not looking.* It is a fact of flying that the same pilots who, while in the air, spot airplanes with the eagerness of a B-17 tailgunner often don't look where they are taxiing. Defensive driving is the key here. Give any airplane with a pilot in the cockpit a wide berth, whether it is moving or not. Expect parked airplanes to pull ahead without clearing, converging traffic to hold an intercept course, and head-on traffic to squeeze you off the taxiway. Taxi accidents don't usually injure people, but even a slight tap is tough on wing tips and wallets, and a close shave plays havoc on the nerves of pilot and passengers alike.

Give passengers a smooth taxi back to the ramp and you will leave them smiling. Begin this smooth taxi with a smooth start from the stopped position. Prevent rough jackrabbit starts. Refrain from gaining rolling momentum with a blast of power. Rather, slowly squeeze in the power with 50 RPM increments from idle until motion starts, then slightly reduce that power for smooth acceleration.

Taxi speed is dependent on runway surface, traffic conditions, and wind. Generally, the slower you taxi, the smoother the ride.

Once under way with taxi speed established, plan ahead to maintain that speed. Anticipate the factors that tend to disturb taxi speed and make small power adjustments before those factors affect your airplane. If a slight uphill grade lies ahead, for example, mash in an extra 50 RPM just before you get to the slope. Or if you see that a turn into the head wind lies ahead, add a few RPMs as you turn into the wind. Anticipate the airplane's needs. This is the difference between maintaining a taxi speed and correcting a taxi speed, the difference between a smooth or rough ride.

Brake sparingly. Use rudder and nosewheel for turning and throttle for decelerating whenever possible. And, of course, pilots should not taxi with their toes resting on the brakes, anymore than they would drive a car with a foot riding the brakes. Riding the brakes is not only hard on the equipment, it is hard on passengers; it usually creates a fishtailing taxi not often felt by the pilot. Pilots sit right over the wheels, the pivot point of the swerving action; the rear seat passenger rides the fishtail.

Leave your passengers smiling. Taxi with an imaginary pan of ice water in your lap.

## Shutting Down

Swing into shutdown position mindful of your prop wash and anything behind you. Try to stop in an area safely away from doorways and walkways. Maintain a constant vigil for pedestrians, with the knowledge that they are probably unaware of your propeller arc. If someone should come to close, don't take the time to kill the engine with the mixture. Just cut the switches; it's a full second quicker in most small airplanes. And, of course, a pilot should never let a passenger deplane until the propeller has stopped.

Pay close attention to your shutdown procedure; it is best

not to talk to passengers. Follow this simple checklist for the shutdown:

1. Set hand brake to prevent unnoticed movement.
2. Turn off electrical and radio equipment.
3. Retract flaps.
4. Close throttle.
5. Move mixture to idle cutoff.
6. Turn off battery switch.
7. Turn off ignition switch and remove key.
8. Install control lock.
9. Release brakes and chock wheels.

Make a rule never to leave a light airplane unchocked. Even a moderate breeze or prop wash from the lightest twin can start your airplane rolling, possibly into another airplane or a building. A mere touch can bring costly repairs.

If your tanks need refueling and you don't know the line attendant, stand by your airplane and monitor the servicing. For all you know, that attendant was hired 20 minutes ago and has never touched an airplane. (Yes, that does happen!) I have watched untrained linemen drag gas hoses across expensive paint; completely overlook a second gas tank; try to pour oil without a spout or a funnel; and make dozens of other annoying, hazardous, or expensive mistakes.

Walk away from the airplane only after it has been methodically shut down, safely secured, and properly serviced.

Perfect landings won't just happen. You must plan them. Then execute that plan in 10 separate steps, each with its own goal, and you stand a very good chance of achieving a perfect and seemingly effortless landing.

# IN REVIEW: Normal Landings

### PREFLIGHT REMINDERS

- Landings begin several miles out with a precision letdown to pattern altitude.
- Use landmarks throughout your landing procedure to help visualize desired ground tracks.
- Use landmarks throughout your landing procedure as intermediate goals to help plan ahead.
- Learn to slow-fly your airplane accurately at approach speed to cope with traffic in the pattern.
- Develop standard procedure for extending flaps.
- Remain constantly aware of wind direction throughout the landing sequence.
- Remember that most midair collisions happen during the landing phase of flight. Use the pattern's legs to spot traffic effectively.
- The secret to a good approach lies in airspeed control, and trim is the key. Retrim with each change in power or flaps.
- Plan your landing procedure as 10 separate steps:

## 1. Descending to the destination airport

- If you have no more than 5000 feet to lose, begin your descent 10 minutes out.
- If you have over 5000 feet to lose, begin your descent 20 minutes out.
- Estimate your rate of descent against either a 10- or 20-minute letdown.
- Descend to a landmark 5 miles from the airport, which puts you in position to enter the downwind leg at a 45-degree angle.
- Begin slowing to gear-extension speed 5 miles out.

## 2. Entering the traffic pattern

- Lower the wheels one-half mile before turning downwind to decelerate to flap-operating range.

- Select landmarks that help you visualize the downwind ground track.
- Slow the airplane to pattern speed.
- Exercise your prelanding checklist.
- Select 'a half-mile final-fix landmark.
- Pick a touchdown target.
- Decide on your go-around point.

3. Flying the traffic pattern

- Plan a pattern of 1.7 × stall.
- Consider using partial flaps for normal landings.
- Anticipate the wind drift on each leg of this traffic pattern.

4. Descending to the runway

- Begin procedure abeam your touchdown target.
- Establish approach speed before reaching base leg.
- Reevaluate your glide path to the half-mile final-fix landmark with each 50-foot increment on the altimeter.
- Use very small throttle movements to maintain a smooth glide path.
- Start using the apparent motion of the touchdown target as you cross the final-fix point.
- If the target appears to move upward or away from you, the glide path is too low.
- If the target appears to move downward or toward you, the glide path is too high.
- Once the apparent motion of the touchdown spot stabilizes, your glide path is on target.

5. Rounding out

- Coordinate your power reduction with your change in pitch attitude so the throttle hits idle just as the tires touch.
- Time your change in pitch attitude so the nose covers the far end of the runway just as the tires touch.

**6.** Touching down

- Deliver a good follow-through. Continue to apply aft stick pressure right through touchdown.
- Use all available stick travel to keep the nosewheel off as long as possible.

**7.** Rolling out

- Keep your vision locked on the center stripes while the airplane is rolling.
- Remember that the airplane is subject to aileron drag or adverse yaw during the roll-out.
- Delay closing the carburetor heat, retracting the flaps, or switching frequencies until the airplane is off the runway and stopped.

**8.** Clearing the runway

- Under normal circumstances, begin braking only after the airplane has coasted to a fast taxi speed.
- Taxi at least 100 feet down the taxiway before stopping.

**9.** Taxiing to the ramp

- Taxi defensively and remember that other pilots are probably not aware of your position.
- Avoid jackrabbit starts and lurching stops.
- Plan ahead and anticipate the factors that tend to disturb taxi speed.
- Avoid taxiing with toes on the brakes.

**10.** Shutting down

- Consider where your prop wash is blowing.
- Remain alert for pedestrians approaching your propeller arc.
- Follow a shutdown checklist.
- Chock the airplane if you plan to leave it.
- Stand by your airplane during servicing.

| CRUISE AIRSPEED | DISTANCE NEEDED 10 MIN. DESCENT | DISTANCE NEEDED 20 MIN. DESCENT |
|---|---|---|
| 90 | 15 mi. | 30 mi. |
| 120 | 20 mi. | 40 mi. |
| 150 | 25 mi. | 50 mi. |
| 180 | 30 mi. | 60 mi. |
| 210 | 35 mi. | 70 mi. |

| ALTITUDE TO LOSE | FPM NEEDED 10 MIN. DESCENT | FPM NEEDED 20 MIN. DESCENT |
|---|---|---|
| 2000 | 200 | |
| 3000 | 300 | |
| 4000 | 400 | |
| 5000 | 500 | |
| 6000 | | 300 |
| 7000 | | 350 |
| 8000 | | 400 |
| 9000 | | 450 |
| 10000 | | 500 |

**Fig. 1.12.** If you have less than 5000 feet to lose to the pattern altitude, start your descent 10 minutes from the destination airport. A descent of more than 5000 feet should start 20 minutes out. Apply the time factor against the altitude to arrive at a value to fly on your vertical speed indicator.

# USEFUL LANDING POWER SETTINGS

## For aircraft _____

| POWER SETTINGS FOR : | RPM | MP |
|---|---|---|
| 55 Percent Power | | |
| Slow-Flight at Approach Speed | | |
| Pattern Speed | | |
| Descent to Runway | | |

## For aircraft _____

| POWER SETTINGS FOR : | RPM | MP |
|---|---|---|
| 55 Percent Power | | |
| Slow-Flight at Approach Speed | | |
| Pattern Speed | | |
| Descent to Runway | | |

**Fig. 1.13.** Enter the information useful to the planes you fly for a quick in-flight reference.

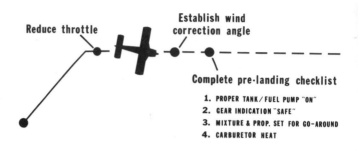

Reduce throttle

Establish wind
correction angle

Complete pre-landing checklist

1. PROPER TANK / FUEL PUMP "ON"
2. GEAR INDICATION "SAFE"
3. MIXTURE & PROP. SET FOR GO-AROUND
4. CARBURETOR HEAT

**Fig. 1.14.** As you enter the downwind leg, reduce the power to pattern speed, pin down the wind drift, and complete your prelanding checklist.

## SIGNIFICANT PATTERN SPEEDS
### For aircraft _____

Gear Extension _____ kts / mph

Flap Extension _____ kts / mph

Downwind Speed _____ kts / mph

Approach Speed _____ kts / mph

### For aircraft _____

Gear Extension _____ kts / mph

Flap Extension _____ kts / mph

Downwind Speed _____ kts / mph

Approach Speed _____ kts / mph

**Fig. 1.15.** Enter the airspeeds that the traffic pattern demands of the planes you fly for a quick prelanding review.

# CHECKLISTS

## BEFORE LANDING

A. FUEL SELECTOR — proper tank
B. GEAR WARNING INDICATOR — test
C. GEAR — down and locked
D. MIXTURE — set for possible go-around
E. PROPELLER — set for possible go-around
F. FLAPS — as required
G. CARBURETOR HEAT — as required
Other _____

## AFTER CLEARING RUNWAY

A. STOP WELL CLEAR OF RUNWAY
B. CARBURETOR HEAT — cold
C. WING FLAPS — retract
D. COWL FLAPS — open
Other _____

## SHUT DOWN

A. BRAKES — set
B. RADIO AND ELECTRICAL ACCESSORIES — off
C. THROTTLE — 800 — 1200 rpm
D. MIXTURE — idle cut-off
E. MASTER SWITCH — off
F. IGNITION SWITCH — off; remove key
G. GUST LOCK — insert
H. BRAKES — release and chock wheels
Other _____

# 2 | Crosswind Procedures

FOR SHEER EXCITEMENT, there are few moments in flying equal to those of a crosswind landing gone wrong. Picture yourself rigid with surprise as you look through the windshield of an airplane at odd angles to the centerline and drifting toward the runway's edge as the tires hit, hearing rubber squealing outside and the sharp inhaling of the passengers inside the slewing cockpit. It's the sort of thing that sends a squirt of adrenalin right out of the pilot's ears and that passengers recount over their supper tables for weeks to come.

The inability to handle crosswinds safely continues to be a leading cause of flying accidents. True, people are rarely injured, but a tattered wing tip can be expensive. If the side-load weight of an uncorrected crosswind touchdown is heavy enough to collapse a gear and let the prop hit with sudden stoppage, a second mortgage is a reasonable possibility.

Crosswind technique is a skill that quickly erodes for two simple reasons, reasons with a cumulative effect on the pilot's crosswind ability. First, the crosswind landing is a complex maneuver to understand and execute. There are many forces for the pilot to juggle simultaneously, and the extremely high degree of control coordination and timing required is seldom matched by any other phase of flight. This means that the pilot must use the crosswind procedure frequently to remain proficient. And the crosswind skill erodes for a second reason: Most pilots wisely elect not to fly in a crosswind that could test their ability to handle it, but the problem still arises when a brisk crosswind develops while the pilot is aloft. So we have two opposing facts of flight. One says we must use it or lose it, and the other, the logic of safety, tells us not to use it when it will do us the most good by testing out skills. No wonder crosswind ability is one of the first skills to get rusty, and this deficiency remains a major cause of bent airplanes.

Let's review some of the basic concepts of crosswind landings, then "follow through" on the execution of a typical crosswind landing, and finally, look at some ways to maintain and further expand crosswind skills.

# Basic Concepts

Making a crosswind landing sounds simple: touch down astride the centerline with the airplane in runway alignment, devoid of sidewise drift, and maintain a crosswind follow-through during roll-out. Most pilots understand very well the *whys* of achieving this four-part goal. They understand, for instance, that a centerline touchdown conserves runway width they may need in the event of an unanticipated swerve and that runways are constructed with a high crest, so any off-center touchdown *invites* a swerve.

They understand, too, that an unwanted side load is imposed against the landing gear unless they touch down with the nose pointed straight ahead and with no side drift to their flight path. These pilots have watched side loads send airplanes toward mishap with chirping bird-hops or hairy skids. Most pilots also understand that they cannot give up the crosswind correction once the tires are down. To do so lets unexpected bumps bounce them sideways rather than glide them straight ahead.

Most pilots, then, understand the *whys* involved in the basic concept of the crosswind landing. It is usually the *hows* that elude them. This is most often caused by misconceptions concerning basic principles of crosswind correction. Let's review some of these basics by looking at seven common areas of misconception.

**AILERONS AND RUDDER.** Many pilots have difficulty coordinating the flight controls in a crosswind. They are bothered not so much by the cross-control nature of the maneuver as they are by the true functions of ailerons and rudder. In reality, each control serves a separate function as the pilot corrects for the crosswind. Ailerons are used to stop any sidewise wind drift, and the rudder is used to keep the airplane's fuselage aligned with the runway. When the pilot uses ailerons to bank into the wind — let's say to the right for a right crosswind — the wing's lift is deflected toward the right, and the force of lift tugs the airplane into the wind. If there is not enough bank for the wind and insufficient lift is deflected to the right for the required "tugging-power," the airplane still drifts sidewise with the wind. If there is too much bank for the crosswind, excess lift is deflected to the right, and the airplane actually moves sidewise against the wind.

Of course, when you bank to the right to prevent drift, the airplane's nose will also turn right unless you do something about it. And that's where opposite rudder comes into the crosswind correction. Rudder is simply used to prevent the airplane from turning toward the direction of the banked wings and to keep the airplane flying straight down the runway, aligned with the centerline.

So a pilot may think of controls as performing separate functions — aileron for sidewise drift and rudder for runway alignment. But many pilots don't know how much of each control to use. This is the simplest decision of all, if you make use of one invaluable visual aid — the centerline painted in the runway.

Most pilots who have difficulty with crosswind controls cannot tell you *why* a centerline is there, which means they usually are not even *aware* of the centerline when landing. This is often the case simply because the centerline is hard to see during the last moments of landing. You must stretch your neck to keep it in sight.

This lack of awareness is the prime source of crosswind difficulty, because that centerline is put there specifically to assist in crosswind landing. It gives you a second-by-second evaluation of your airplane's wind drift and runway alignment. Picture landing in a right crosswind, with the centerline in sight. If you start to drift left of the line, you know you must increase aileron. If, on the other hand, you move right (against the wind) you know you must decrease aileron pressure. And if you see the nose cocked to the right of centerline, you must increase "opposite rudder." If the nose points to the left, you must decrease "opposite-rudder" pressure.

Use the centerline stripe to evaluate the magnitude of your aileron and rudder deflections — crosswind control is as simple as that.

**CAPRICIOUS WIND.** Oftentimes when descending on final, a pilot corrects for the crosswind and then counts on that correction to hold until touchdown. This seldom works, however. Wind is a fickle force. It rarely blows at a constant velocity or direction, and you must stay nimble with ailerons and rudder right through touchdown and roll-out. Even a quick glance at the wind sock is of little value during the round-out and touchdown. It is usually too far away, and several puffs of wind change it between the letdown and the landing zone, where exactness counts. The centerline, however, tells you everything you need to know about wind conditions on an instant-to-instant basis.

**EFFECT OF GROUNDSPEED.** A landing pilot flies the airplane through a range of airspeeds that varies from approach speed to near stall speed. This means, of course, that ground speed changes considerably as the airplane is brought down to the runway. Many pilots are not aware of the significant impact ground speed makes on the crosswind correction required. The slower an airplane moves over the ground, the greater the crosswind effect becomes. This interaction of wind force and time means that the pilot can expect to increase control deflections as the airplane slows to touchdown speed. Again, the white centerline tells the story.

**UPRAISED TIRE.** Most pilots know that they are supposed to touch down on the upwind tire. But some think that they must then level their wings to lower the raised tire. Nothing could be further from the truth. This moment of transition — when the airplane is part flying machine and part ground machine — is especially critical for proper crosswind control. The pilot must keep aileron pressure through the touchdown and increase control deflection while continuing to decelerate. Forget about the upraised tire. The weight of the aircraft brings it down when the time is right.

**AILERON DRAG.** Again, picture landing with the crosswind blowing from the right. After touchdown and during roll-out, the wind pushes against the right side of the vertical stabilizer and tries to weather-vane the airplane to the right. Keep the right aileron deflected because *aileron drag* will help you roll straight ahead (Fig. 2.1). With the control wheel deflected to the right, the left aileron extends below the wing and digs into the air. The right aileron, of course, lifts and is protected from the onrushing air by the wing's curved upper surface. As the airplane's roll slows, apply more and more control deflection to maintain the left aileron's "digging power." Proper aileron movement during roll-out achieves full control deflection just as the airplane rolls to a stop. It is practically impossible to use too much aileron during this segment of a landing.

---

**Fig. 2.1.** This photo during the roll-out displays aileron drag. With the crosswind blowing from the left, the pilot has lowered his right aileron into the slipstream. The left aileron is protected from the slipstream by the wing's curved upper surface.

**GO-AROUND.** The possible go-around is an integral part of crosswind landing procedure. Yet few pilots include this safety margin in their crosswind plans.

Most modern, single engine, light airplanes are capable of delivering a go-around from the touchdown attitude. Pilots, however, may need review instruction in the technique; and if so, they should get it. Unless your airplane is landing astride the centerline, aligned with the runway and free of drift, you should consider executing a go-around. Doing so may spare your airplane from the damage of a crosswind accident. If all pilots would include a possible go-around in their crosswind procedure, landing accidents would be virtually eliminated.

**TAXIING DOWNWIND.** Should you hold the ailerons into or away from the wind when taxiing with a strong quartering tail wind? This can be a confusing question until you understand what is actually happening with wind and ailerons. Many pilots are not sure about the forces at work. A common explanation is that "the wing is flying backward," which is, of course, nowhere near the truth, since the wing is not even an airfoil in this situation. It's merely a chunk of metal with wind blowing against it.

To envision the forces at work during a quartering tail wind taxi, picture taxiing back to the ramp with a strong wind blowing from the right rear. Your problem is to prevent the wind from catching under the right aileron and lifting the right wing tip. The downwind wing tip is of no concern. The wind cannot catch it with sufficient strength to roll the plane against the force of the wind. Now, with the wind blowing from behind, which looks logical? To deflect the aileron upward? Or downward? Downward, naturally, so the wind cannot get under it. When making control deflections as you taxi, forget about diagrams that tell you which way to turn the control wheel. Just look out at the upwind wing tip and picture how the wind is blowing across it; then look at that aileron and simply deflect it in the direction that makes the best sense.

## Crosswind Technique

There are three generally accepted methods for handling the crosswind landing: the crab, the slip, and the combination crab/slip.

The pilot using the crab method establishes a wind-correction angle (or crab) on final, and maintains a drift-free descent in this manner until the moment of touchdown. At the exact instant before the tires touch, the airplane is whipped into runway alignment and lands, without side drift and with the nose pointed straight down the centerline.

All of this, however, presupposes three facts. First, that the wind will behave itself and not shift in the moment before touchdown. Second, that the pilot has enough experience to know exactly when the tires are going to touch. And finally, that the pilot has the skill to guarantee a no-bounce landing.

A gust of wind in the moment when you have straightened the tires to touch will drift the airplane and impose a side load on the gear. If you cannot predict the exact instant of touchdown, you are again very apt to impose a side load on the gear. If you straighten out too soon, the airplane drifts; if you straighten out too late, the airplane lands in the crab. Either mistake imposes a side load. In the event of a bounced landing there is very little time to reestablish the crab. The airplane drifts immediately and relands with a side load against the landing gear. Unless the pilot is very skilled, the crosswind crab method can be dangerous.

The slip technique also has a shortcoming, but it is one of discomfort rather than hazard. The pilot employing this method establishes the slip well out on final and corrects for the wind with that slip right on through touchdown. It is a relatively easy and effective technique, but it's uncomfortable for passengers. While descending toward the ground in a slanting cockpit, you may feel only mild discomfort — but then you know what's going on. Passengers, on the other hand, usually widen their eyes considerably, particularly if the direction of the slip leans them against the door. They can only surmise that you have suddenly lost control or equilibrium, and they are very apt to make gurgling noises. As they look through the askew windshield at the uprushing ground, they will probably reckon the rest of their lives in terms of the unwinding altimeter.

For this reason, most pilots prefer to use a combination crab/slip method. It is safe, easy to perform, and gets the job done. To use this technique, establish a crab early in the final leg, holding the drift with a wind-correction angle until beginning to round out. As you round out, lower a wing into the wind and use opposite rudder to hold the airplane's nose straight down the centerline. This slip is held right through touchdown. Small changes in the magnitude of the slip can be made quickly to allow for any sudden wind shift. It is unnecessary for you to know exactly when the tires are going to touch; simply hold the touchdown attitude until they do. And if a bounce occurs, the ailerons are already doing their job to ensure that the airplane floats straight ahead.

Let's follow the action as you conduct a typical crosswind landing. The wind is blowing from right to left, and your airplane has just completed the turn from base to final. When you pass over the half-mile final-fix landmark, eyeball a projected flight path in alignment with the centerline. A quick trial wind-correction angle is made into the wind. From this point on, keep the flight path in straight alignment with the runway, using the centerline as your main visual reference. If the airplane drifts downwind, to the left, add a few degrees of correction. If the airplane begins to move upwind of runway alignment, decrease the correction a few degrees. The typical error made here is overcorrection. Limit any changes in crab angle to a few degrees. This is particularly important when the airplane is upwind from centerline alignment. In this case, reduce the correction two or three degrees and let the wind drift the airplane back on course.

As the airplane descends over the threshold, begin to reduce airspeed. Lift the nose slightly, cut back on throttle, and retrim. At this point ease from the crab into the slip. Bank slightly toward the wind and bring the airplane's nose into centerline alignment with opposite rudder. Nimble readjustments of aileron and rudder are needed to pin down the wind. Close attention to the runway centerline gives immediate information; the aileron stops drift; the rudder keeps the fuselage pointed straight down the runway. The airplane continually slows toward its landing speed as it closes to touchdown. And with each reduction in ground speed, the pilot needs to increase the magnitude of slip.

When the airplane attains the touchdown attitude, it has reached its slowest flying speed. It is at this slow ground speed that the airplane is most susceptible to even the slightest puff of wind. The pilot must pay very close attention to the centerline and make the appropriate control deflections quickly — aileron for drift, rudder for alignment.

The moment the upwind tire touches, speed dissipates further. The airplane is now part flying machine and part ground machine. Continue to increase aileron deflection in case of bounce and maintain the centerline with rudder control.

Continue to add aileron even after the second tire sets down on the runway. Aileron drag helps keep the airplane from weather-vaning into the wind. Continue to increase aileron throughout the landing roll, reaching maximum control deflection just as the airplane rolls to a stop. This concludes the crosswind landing.

## Expanding Your Crosswind Skill

As pilots, we must continually strive to improve our skills. They either get better or they get worse; they rarely remain unchanged. And, as we have seen, crosswind landing technique is a skill highly susceptible to erosion.

If your crosswind skills have already receded to minimum, your first step is clear. After reviewing the basic concepts and techniques, you need a session of dual instruction to bring your skills back to average.

Consider these three avenues of recurrent training to hone your talent:

1. Crosswind control drills at altitude.
2. Solo practice landings in significant crosswinds.
3. Dual instruction in winds beyond your present ability.

**DRILLS AT ALTITUDE.** It is no wonder that, as student pilots, we had trouble learning the control coordination demanded by crosswind landings. With each landing we were exposed to unique and complex control movements for only a few seconds, during which our minds were diverted elsewhere — gritting our teeth with pitch and throttle control, trying to hear the instructor over engine and radio chatter, puckering in anticipation that the uprushing runway would smack us. We really had neither the time nor the opportunity to learn crosswind control.

But crosswind drill at altitude is a method of learning this control in relaxed comfort. Here's how it works: Pick out a long road or similar straight line that lies crosswind. At 2000 feet above the road, establish a wind-correction angle that prevents drift. Then throttle back and let your airplane descend along the road. Ease from the crab into the slip, using the road as a centerline. You have a good 2 minutes to play with the crosswind, completely relaxed. Level off at 1000 feet above the road, climb to your starting altitude, reverse direction, and practice with the opposite crosswind.

Most pilots make an important discovery during this drill. They find that they have not been using nearly enough opposite rudder during their crosswind corrections, a fairly common shortcoming. As you try the drill, experiment with twice the rudder pressure you feel necessary. Make the discovery!

**SOLO PRACTICE.** Every pilot should devote several practice sessions each year to crosswind landings. When the crosswind is moderate or near the limit of your skill, make the flights your solo practice. But heed two cautions. First, prepare yourself by practicing go-arounds from the landing attitude and be mentally prepared to do so anytime you suspect a bad touchdown; and, second, practice crosswind landings when a brisk crosswind exists at a neighboring airport and make landings there, leaving your home airport with the wind fairly well down the runway. Otherwise, if the wind increases during your solo practice, the crosswind may exceed your ability, and you may find yourself practicing 3 hours of go-arounds instead of crosswind landings. When you do encounter a crosswind beyond your ability, it is best not to fight it. Fly to another airport with a more favorable runway, land there, and wait it out.

**DUAL INSTRUCTION.** The most practical way to increase your crosswind skill is to practice in winds that exceed your present ability. And the only safe way to do this is with a flight instructor, even though it is usually difficult to schedule this sort of training flight. Usually, you have to wait for high wind and call your instructor for an on-the-spot appointment. Make sure your instructor is thoroughly familiar with the airplane you intend to use. Letting you practice crosswind landings beyond your ability produces tense moments for the instructor, which are tolerable if the absolute limits of the airplane are known.

A word of advice: If the airplane you normally fly is one of the complex "heavyweights" of the light airplane field, consider practicing in a strong crosswind first with a light trainer type. After you've mastered the technique, move on into your larger, complex airplane. Bonanzas, Centurions, and the like are not really meant for the rigors of the trial and error involved in expanding crosswind skill.

# IN REVIEW: Crosswind Procedures

PREFLIGHT REMINDERS

- Four-part goal:
  1. Touchdown astride centerline.
  2. Plane aligned with centerline.
  3. No side drift.
  4. Crosswind follow-through.

- Ailerons are used to stop side drift.
- Rudder is used to keep the airplane aligned with the runway.
- Use the centerline as a visual aid.
- Remember that the wind rarely blows at a constant direction and velocity.
- Remember that the slower the ground speed, the greater the crosswind effect.
- Realize that the moment of touchdown is especially critical for crosswind correction.
- Use aileron drag to prevent the airplane from weather-vaning during roll-out.
- Include the possible go-around as an integral part of crosswind procedure.
- When taxiing with a quartering tail wind, deflect the upwind aileron so the wind cannot catch under it.
- Begin crosswind correction as you cross the half-mile final-fix point.
- Limit any changes in crab angle to a few degrees.
- Change from the crab to the slip as you break your glide speed.
- Maintain a crosswind correction until the airplane stops moving.
- Avenues of recurrent training:

    1. Crosswind drills at altitude.
    2. Solo practice.
    3. Dual instruction.

## CROSS-WIND COMPONENTS

| ANGLE OF WIND TO RUNWAY | WIND VELOCITY AS X-W COMPONENT |
|---|---|
| 30 degrees | ½ wind velocity |
| 45 degrees | ⅔ wind velocity |
| 60 degrees | ¾ wind velocity |

**PERSONAL MAXIMUM X-W COMPONENT :____KTS.**

**Fig. 2.2.** To use this table as a quick prelanding reference, simply compare the estimated crosswind component to your own "maximum."

## PRELANDING CROSS-WIND REMINDERS

1. TOUCH DOWN ASTRIDE CENTERLINE.
2. TOUCH DOWN ALIGNED WITH CENTERLINE.
3. TOUCH DOWN WITH NO SIDE DRIFT.
4. FOLLOW THROUGH WITH X-W CORRECTION.
5. KEEP THE GO-AROUND OPTION IN MIND.

**Fig. 2.3.** A quick prelanding reference to a crosswind landing checklist could prevent an accident.

# 3 | Short-Field Operations

PLAN YOUR APPROACH to the short runway with all the caution and cunning of a pro quarterback committed to a fourth-down pass from his own end zone. Keep in mind two reasons that short fields have produced more than their fair share of accidents in recent years: Most of today's pilots receive their training on long, paved, well-maintained runways, and most of today's airplanes are designed to operate from these same runways. Plan your short-field procedures to recognize these two facts of flying. Develop a good procedure that provides fail-safe measures to stop the action when a hazardous situation emerges; one that also provides a series of "outs" for the inexperienced short-field pilot or the airplane ill equipped for short-field landings.

## Aircraft Performance

Begin your defensive short-field procedure by following a rule of thumb: Consult the airplane's landing distance chart any time the runway length is less than 3000 feet, the field elevation exceeds 2500 feet, or the temperature exceeds 85° F.

Remember, though, that most landing charts assume normal conditions exist — a dry, paved level runway, for example. But the landing strip you face may pose any number of *abnormal* factors. So study the landing chart and its variables to ferret out factors that must be modified to your short field.

Here are some landing chart variables, and a few thoughts on how they relate to the runway you actually face (Fig. 3.1).

Fig. 3.1.

---

**EIGHT VARIABLES EFFECTING LANDING DISTANCE**

1. RUNWAY SURFACE
2. FLAPS AND AIRSPEED
3. FIELD ELEVATION
4. GROSS WEIGHT
5. HEADWIND COMPONENT
6. TEMPERATURE
7. OBSTACLE CLEARANCE
8. PILOT TECHNIQUE

**RUNWAY SURFACE.** The aircraft manual's landing distance is often stated for a paved braking surface only. Short fields, however, are unpaved more often than not. As a rule of thumb, add 20 percent to the stated distance for dry grass or turf and 50 percent if the ground is wet.

**FLAPS AND AIRSPEED.** The manufacturer's estimate of landing distance normally assumes the use of full flaps and the recommended approach speed. In executing a short-field landing, you should touch down at the slowest ground speed your airplane safely allows. This, of course, helps produce the minimum possible ground roll. To accomplish this, extend full flaps after you are established on final and slow the airplane to the lowest approach speed recommended by the manufacturer.

Full flaps and the slowest safe approach speed also result in a relatively steep approach. This descent consumes the least amount of runway length, particularly if you are letting down over an obstacle.

**FIELD ELEVATION.** Fly your approach at the manufacturer's recommended *indicated* airspeed, regardless of field elevation. Your *true* airspeed is, of course, slightly higher at the higher elevations. This results in a greater ground speed at touchdown and hence a longer landing roll. If your airplane's landing chart does not include various elevations, use this rule of thumb: increase the sea-level landing distance by 5 percent for each 1000 feet of elevation. Remember that high elevation landings (over 5000 feet) may call for a leaned mixture on final to make a go-around possible.

**AIRCRAFT GROSS WEIGHT.** The heavier an airplane is loaded, the greater the rolling momentum and the longer the stopping distance. If the manufacturer's charts specify only maximum allowable gross weight landing distances, then use this rule of thumb for the lightly loaded aircraft: reduce the required distance by 5 percent for each 100 pounds under the maximum allowable gross weight. You may also reduce your approach speed by 1 mile per hour for each 100 pounds under maximum gross weight to achieve a slower touchdown speed. If you do not reduce approach speed accordingly, your plane may "float" on landing and the landing distance will probably increase.

**HEAD WIND COMPONENT.** Each 10 knots of head wind generally shortens the no-wind landing distance by 20 percent. To estimate the head wind component, overfly the runway and look at the wind sock. It takes 15 knots to stiffen the sock, so if it is hanging at a 45-degree droop, the breeze is about 7 to 8 knots. If the sock is swinging within 30 degrees of runway alignment, consider there is a direct head wind. Allow half the wind's velocity as a head wind component when the sock swings 30 to 60 degrees off the runway. And when the sock's angle with the runway exceeds 60 degrees, count the head wind zero.

A few strips are considered "one-way" runways; that is, regardless of wind, landings are made in only one direction. In these cases, be sure to increase the landing roll accordingly if any tail wind component exists.

**TEMPERATURE.** In the absence of manual information, use this rule of thumb: Add 10 percent of the landing distance for each 40° F above the standard temperature for the field elevation. (Standard temperature is 59° F at sea level and decreases about 10° F for each 2500 feet.) To estimate the runway temperature, look at your outside air temperature gauge and add 4° F for each 1000 feet down to field elevation.

**OBSTACLE CLEARANCE.** Aircraft landing charts usually express required distance in two forms: ground roll and total-to-clear-obstacle. Ground roll is the appropriate distance it takes to brake the airplane to a stop once it has touched down. The total-to-clear-obstacle distance contemplates an approach over a 50-foot-high obstruction near the end of the runway. This distance provides the approximate total needed to descend over the obstacle to a touchdown point and bring the airplane to a stop. In reality, this is very nearly like the glide path we make even when no obstacles exist. So it is this figure — total-to-clear-obstacle — that is of paramount value to the pilot considering the safety of the landing. Unless you are very, very good or the need to land is desperate, do not land unless the runway length provides 150 percent of the total-to-clear-obstacle distance for the prevailing landing conditions. This safety margin is needed to prevent an unexpected overrun caused by a situation beyond the pilot's control, such as a wet patch of grass, a downgrade near the runway's end, a sudden loss of head wind, or no brakes. As an example, consider landing a fully loaded Skyhawk at a sea-level grass field on a hot windless afternoon. The landing chart calls for about 1600 feet total distance. Unless that runway exceeds 2400 feet (1600 × 1.5) or you are an ace, *don't* try it.

**PILOT TECHNIQUE.** This is the last and most important of the landing chart variables. The aircraft manufacturer has based projections for the airplane's performance on the assumption that the pilot exercises average ability. I'm not sure exactly what average means, but I do know this: if your proposed flight includes a landing at a short field, honestly evaluate your ability to handle it. And if you have any doubts, obtain some instruction in short-field technique before you set out.

# Regulations and Preflight Planning

Research your airplane's performance and your destination's runway conditions *before* you depart, not as you're descending to the airport. Not only is this preflight activity good procedure but federal regulations mandate it. FAR 91.5, *Preflight Action,* reads in part: "Each pilot in command shall, before beginning a flight, familiarize himself with all available information concerning that flight. This information must include . . . runway lengths of intended use . . . and flight manual take-off and landing distance data . . . aircraft performance under expected values of airport elevation and runway slope, aircraft weight, and wind and temperature."

The pilot's preflight weather briefing can disclose the destination wind and temperature that are expected at the time of arrival. Runway surface and length, field elevation, and runway heading (to estimate an anticipated head wind or crosswind component) can be found in the *Airport/Facility Directory* or on the sectional chart.

Pilots flying to an unfamiliar airport denoted R on the sectional chart should anticipate possible adverse runway conditions. A briefing from a pilot who knows the field or a long-distance call to the field itself may give you invaluable information.

## Short-Field Procedures and Pilot Technique

Begin your short-field procedure with a slow-flight overfly of the strip, 500 feet above pattern altitude. Look hard for company, then study the runway surface. Note activities on the field (mowers, gliders, etc.) and estimate your head wind component from the wind sock. While still above the airport, pick two marks on the runway that ensure accuracy and safety — your touchdown target and your go-around point.

A pilot must keep a definite touchdown target in sight to prevent undershooting or overshooting the landing. Choose a mark about a third of the way down the runway. This is far enough to prevent a misjudgment from letting you land short or clip a fence, yet it is near enough to the threshold to conserve adequate runway for touchdown and roll-out. On sod or turf strips, that worn patch where the local pilots touch makes a good bull's eye. Without a visible touchdown target, you may not recognize a poor glide path until you are nearly down, and your last-second bid with flaps or power is bound to produce an uncontrolled and unsafe landing.

It is just as important to choose a visible go-around point. A definite point at which you must execute a go-around is the only guarantee you have that the landing will not end with a bent airplane and that adequate braking distance will remain after the wheels touch down.

Select your go-around point as a mark halfway down the runway. If your overall runway length exceeds 150 percent of the required total-to-clear-obstacle distance, half the runway length will normally provide an adequate safe stopping distance. On unpaved runways, a mark on the runway conveniently at midpoint usually does not exist. More often than not you must be satisfied with a mark alongside the runway (parked plane, wind sock, building, etc.). However, you do need some visible go-around point. Decide while you are overflying the airport to automatically execute a go-around if your tires haven't touched by the time your go-around point zips by. When dealing with a short runway, you cannot leave that critical decision to those last few tense seconds while you are skimming along the rapidly diminishing runway length.

After you have made an overhead scan of the runway, turn toward a landmark 2 or 3 miles away so you can enter the downwind leg at a 45-degree angle. Descend to the pattern altitude as you fly outbound, and once again scout the area for traffic as you fly back toward the airport. As you approach the downwind leg, mentally trace the ground track you want your pattern to follow. Beware though; many pilots erroneously scale down the size of their pattern when landing at a short field. This error usually produces a time-shortened approach that ends up with a high, fast final leg. Trace out the same pattern you use at Bigtown Municipal.

Turn the downwind and set your throttle back to approach speed. Be sure to retrim with each power reduction, and have the airplane at approach speed before you turn base leg. This slows the action and helps a pilot's thinking stay ahead of the airplane.

While flying on the downwind leg, pick the remaining land-mark that you need for your short-field procedure, the final-approach fix. Choose a landmark on final that lies a half-mile from your touchdown target. To quickly estimate a half-mile final, just compare the distance to the known runway length. If, for example, the runway beneath you is 2000 to 3000 feet long, then a half-mile landmark lies about one runway length out.

Plan to cross your half-mile final-fix point at 400 feet AGL. This ensures a fairly accurate glide path that is neither embarrassingly high nor dangerously low. Small power adjustments should be all that is necessary to correct for the variations in normal head winds. You eliminate the need for a power-off, ton-of-bricks descent or a full-power, plant-it-on-the-carrier-deck approach.

Turn to the base leg and consider the two procedures you must mobilize in executing a short-field landing:

1. You must slightly steepen your approach path once any obstacles are safely behind you. This produces a short final that consumes the least amount of runway. You should start a smooth and steady power reduction as the plane passes over the obstacle. A perfect rate of throttle reduction achieves zero thrust just as the wheels touch.
2. You must touch down at the slowest safe ground speed. This produces the shortest possible ground roll. You can best bring this about by extending full flaps after turning final and slowing the airspeed to the lowest approach speed that the aircraft manufacturer recommends.

While still on base leg, lower half the flaps your wings have to offer and retrim with each flap increment. Airspeed is easier to control in a properly trimmed airplane, and distractions do not result in an unexpected nose-down or nose-up attitude during your approach. Set your throttle at 1500 to 1700 RPM and fly a shallow turn that puts you on final slightly outside your final-fix landmark. Continue to evaluate your rate of descent with each 50-foot decrease on the altimeter as you close the distance to that landmark and use small throttle movements to cross the fix at 400 feet AGL.

Turn final, fully extend the flaps as you cross the final-fix landmark, and trim to the airplane's slowest recommended approach speed. Then shift your attention to the touchdown target and use small power variations to maintain an accurate descent. Use a time-tested visual reference to evaluate your approach path. If your touchdown target appears to drift downward or toward you, the glide path is too high; you are overshooting. Conversely, if the target appears to move upward or away from you, you are undershooting. But if the point appears motionless, you will touch down nearly on target.

If obstacle clearance is a factor, use another visual reference to assure clearance. After you have established your approach path, look at your touchdown target and then at the tip of the obstacle lying between you and that target. As long as the apparent vertical distance between the obstacle tip and the target is increasing, you will clear the obstacle. If, however, that gap is diminishing, you may not have clearance (Fig. 3.2).

---

**Fig. 3.2.** As long as the apparent vertical gap between the obstacle's tip and your target on the runway is increasing, you will clear the obstacle. If that gap is diminishing, however, you may not have clearance.

Keep your mind ready for a possible go-around from the moment you start the descent over your half-mile final-approach fix. Several occurrences can make a pull-up advisable. An uncorrected crosswind is certainly grounds for a go-around, as are pedestrians or vehicles that wander onto the runway or a taxiing airplane that arouses your suspicion. A pilot is wise to add power and go-around any time a *large* power change or flap application is needed to correct a glide-path error. A desperate bid with flaps or throttle on short final spoils even the expert's landing, and it may lead to a damaged airplane. Without question, you must pull up if your wheels are not on the ground by the time your go-around point whizzes by. So stay mentally prepared for a go-around as you descend to the runway.

In fact, when landing at an unfamiliar short field, I plan my first approach to the runway as a go-around. I feel that planning a deliberate go-around lends three safety factors to my short-field procedure. First, it gives me a practice shot at a landing technique that I don't often have a chance to use, since most of my flying is from long paved runways. Second, a preplanned go-around makes the idea of an emergency pull-up on the second pass mentally acceptable. Many pilots come to regret a short field just because they hesitated to make the go-around that their logic told them they needed. Vanity, fixation, mental inflexibility — whatever the reason for ignoring that logic, the results are the same. Finally, a deliberate go-around lets me take a close look at what may be a questionable runway surface. Debris, rough areas, and soft spots are more easily spotted on a low pass than they are from pattern altitude. For these reasons, I feel that an intentional go-around is worth the effort. Just be sure to tell your passengers beforehand what you have in mind.

After you touch down on a short runway, keep your eyes straight ahead; short runways are usually on the narrow side. If you look inside the cockpit for a flap handle, carburetor heat knob, or cowl control, you are bound to swerve. If the runway is unpaved, hold full-aft stick during roll-out and taxi to help smooth out the ride.

## Recognizing the Need for Short-Field Technique

Are short-field procedures confined to landings on runways of limited length? Absolutely not. Use the procedures anytime your available landing distance is limited. Examples are easily found in our day-in, day-out flying from long paved strips. The tower imposes a short field on you, for instance, when they instruct you to stop short of an intersecting runway. A large airplane landing on an intersecting runway reduces your available landing distance since you must either land short of that wake turbulence or touch down beyond the vortices. Poor braking surface can shorten the effective distance of an otherwise lengthy runway. A pilot facing a rain-slick runway, for example, would be wise to use short-field procedures and technique, as would a pilot who catches a whiff of hydraulic fluid on downwind and suspects bad brakes. Learn the logic of short-field operations. Practice the procedures and the technique until you are comfortable with them. Then use your short-field plan of action any time you are concerned with bringing the airplane down to rest within the runway length available for your landing.

# IN REVIEW: Short-Field Operations

## PREFLIGHT REMINDERS

- Consult the airplane's landing distance chart any time the runway length is less than 3000 feet, the field elevation exceeds 2500 feet, or the temperature exceeds 85° F.
- The aircraft manual's landing distance may be stated only for a paved runway surface.
- Use full flaps to achieve the slowest safe forward speed and a steep approach.
- If the wind is within 30 degrees of runway alignment, consider it a direct head wind. Allow half the wind's velocity as a head wind component when it lies from 30 to 60 degrees off the runway. Do not allow for any head wind if the wind's angle to the runway exceeds 60 degrees.
- The total-to-clear-obstacle distance provides for a normal approach path.
- Do not land unless the runway provides 150 percent of the total-to-clear obstacle distance for the prevailing conditions.
- If you doubt your short-field skill, get some refresher training before heading to a short-field destination.
- By regulation, you must research the destination's runway situation as it pertains to your airplane's capability.
- A pilot must make go-around plans while still on the downwind leg.
- While on final, use a visual clue to evaluate obstacle clearance. As long as the gap between the tip of the obstacle and the touchdown target is increasing, clearance is assured.
- Stay mentally prepared for a go-around.
- Consider making your first approach a deliberate go-around.
- Use your short-field procedure any time your available landing distance is limited, regardless of the runway's overall length.

# LANDING PERFORMANCE

AIRCRAFT _____

FLAP POSITION _____

APPROACH SPEED _____

## DISTANCES TO CLEAR A 50 FOOT OBSTACLE

**At sea level :**

| GROSS WEIGHT | HEAD WIND | PAVED RUNWAY | | | GRASS RUNWAY | | |
|---|---|---|---|---|---|---|---|
| | | 59° F. | 85° F. | ABORT | 59° F. | 85° F. | ABORT |
| MAX. ALLOW. | 0 | | | | | | |
| | 10 Kt. | | | | | | |
| | 20 Kt. | | | | | | |
| OTHER: ___ lbs. | 0 | | | | | | |
| | 10 Kt. | | | | | | |
| | 20 Kt. | | | | | | |

**At 2500 feet :**

| GROSS WEIGHT | HEAD WIND | PAVED RUNWAY | | | GRASS RUNWAY | | |
|---|---|---|---|---|---|---|---|
| | | 48° F. | 85° F. | ABORT | 48° F. | 85° F. | ABORT |
| MAX. ALLOW. | 0 | | | | | | |
| | 10 Kt. | | | | | | |
| | 20 Kt. | | | | | | |
| OTHER: ___ lbs. | 0 | | | | | | |
| | 10 Kt. | | | | | | |
| | 20 Kt. | | | | | | |

**At 5000 feet :**          (Go-around fuel flow _____ )

| GROSS WEIGHT | HEAD WIND | PAVED RUNWAY | | | GRASS RUNWAY | | |
|---|---|---|---|---|---|---|---|
| | | 38° F. | 85° F. | ABORT | 38° F. | 85° F. | ABORT |
| MAX. ALLOW. | 0 | | | | | | |
| | 10 Kt. | | | | | | |
| | 20 Kt. | | | | | | |
| OTHER: ___ lbs. | 0 | | | | | | |
| | 10 Kt. | | | | | | |
| | 20 Kt. | | | | | | |

**Fig. 3.3** Complete these tables of typical landing conditions for a quick estimation of your plane's landing performance.

# LANDING PERFORMANCE

**AIRCRAFT** _____

**FLAP POSITION** _____

**APPROACH SPEED** _____

## DISTANCES TO CLEAR A 50 FOOT OBSTACLE

### At sea level :

| GROSS WEIGHT | HEAD WIND | PAVED RUNWAY | | | GRASS RUNWAY | | |
|---|---|---|---|---|---|---|---|
| | | 59°F. | 85°F. | ABORT | 59°F. | 85°F. | ABORT |
| MAX. ALLOW. | 0 | | | | | | |
| | 10 Kt. | | | | | | |
| | 20 Kt. | | | | | | |
| OTHER: ____ lbs. | 0 | | | | | | |
| | 10 Kt. | | | | | | |
| | 20 Kt. | | | | | | |

### At 2500 feet :

| GROSS WEIGHT | HEAD WIND | PAVED RUNWAY | | | GRASS RUNWAY | | |
|---|---|---|---|---|---|---|---|
| | | 48°F. | 85°F. | ABORT | 48°F. | 85°F. | ABORT |
| MAX. ALLOW. | 0 | | | | | | |
| | 10 Kt. | | | | | | |
| | 20 Kt. | | | | | | |
| OTHER: ____ lbs. | 0 | | | | | | |
| | 10 Kt. | | | | | | |
| | 20 Kt. | | | | | | |

### At 5000 feet :    (Go-around fuel flow _____)

| GROSS WEIGHT | HEAD WIND | PAVED RUNWAY | | | GRASS RUNWAY | | |
|---|---|---|---|---|---|---|---|
| | | 38°F. | 85°F. | ABORT | 38°F. | 85°F. | ABORT |
| MAX. ALLOW. | 0 | | | | | | |
| | 10 Kt. | | | | | | |
| | 20 Kt. | | | | | | |
| OTHER: ____ lbs. | 0 | | | | | | |
| | 10 Kt. | | | | | | |
| | 20 Kt. | | | | | | |

# 4 | Soft-Field Operations

Fig. 4.1

TODAY'S MODERN AIRPLANES require you to use a special technique for landing on the soft (or rough) airstrips of yesteryear. Today's engines, wings, and propellers are more than adequate for a soft field, certainly far more efficient than those of the airplanes of old. It's the underpinnings that hand us the soft-field problem. Today's small wheels are exactly the right size to drop into any rut that crosses their paths, and the tricycle gear carries us level, shoveling the nosewheel plowshare ahead of us through the rough.

Yesterday's high-stepping Wacos and Jennys, however, sported wheels that could have come right off the axle of a Model T. Those tires just stomped over the ruts and mud holes (Fig. 4.1). They held props high and away from danger, and the uptilted wings provided lift, even at taxi speed.

## Basic Procedure

Even though the soft field does not affect the landing airplane until it reaches the ground, soft-field procedure begins one-half mile out on final. Your letdown must anticipate the soft or rough surface. You must descend to the runway with a minimum sink rate, and your airplane's slowest safe approach speed (Fig. 4.2). The minimum sink rate delivers a light touchdown and prevents the main gear from driving into the soft surface like a couple of fence posts. A minimum approach speed results in the slowest forward motion. It reduces the tendency for the airplane to pitch nose down ,on landing. This minimizes excess drag from the nosewheel, which can easily dip a propeller tip against the rough surface.

---

**THE SOFT-FIELD PROCEDURE MUST ACHIEVE:**

1. A MINIMUM SINK RATE
2. THE SLOWEST SAFE APPROACH SPEED

---

**Fig. 4.2.**

You can achieve a minimum sink rate on landing by carrying a small amount of power right through touchdown. About 1500 RPM or 15 inches manifold pressure is appropriate for most light airplanes. Deliver the slowest speed by extending full flaps and trimming the airplane to the minimum approach speed recommended by the airplane's handbook. If this information is not available, a rule of thumb will suffice: Multiply the lower airspeed of the indicator's white arc by 1.3.

## Soft-Field Technique

Put your soft-field techniques into play 400 feet above your half-mile final-fix point at the airplane's normal approach speed. Once across the final fix, extend full flaps and trim to the airplane's minimum safe descent speed. Since you want to land with some power remaining, delay any throttle reduction until further down the glide path. The combination of full flaps and your normal letdown power setting should produce a workable initial descent slope. Reduce your throttle to the desired touch-down power setting (about 1500 RPM) midway from the final fix to your touchdown target. Quickly evaluate your approach path. If it appears correct as the runway threshold draws near, continue your descent. But if you appear to be either undershooting or overshooting, it is advisable to effect an early go-around. Remember that your airplane is flying extremely slow and the flaps are fully extended, complicating a go-around. As you apply go-around power, the unusually slow speed magnifies the left-turning force of the torque, and the extended flaps exaggerate the upward pitching moment.

Leave your throttle "as is" right through touchdown and use a smooth follow-through to bring the stick back to the stop. Continue your roll-out with the stick fully aft and the throttle at partial power. If possible, keep your throttle setting constant and let the soft ground decelerate your airplane. Decrease flaps to a partial setting. This moves them away from any debris while still producing lift.

Maintain your stick pressure, power, and partial flaps as you turn toward the parking area. The stick-back position and partial power together produce the soft-field taxiing technique. The extra power will help pull your airplane through the soft surface, and the prop blast across the deflected elevator helps lessen the nosewheel's drag against the ground. Don't stop until you reach a firm surface, if possible. Plan ahead and try to avoid the very softest or roughest patches. If you do see a mushy spot that you cannot avoid, be ready to increase power to maintain a constant taxi speed. It is advisable, however, to limit taxi power to 2000 RPM or 20 inches of manifold pressure. Higher power settings often produce an erratic taxi that can lead to a damaged gear or prop. If you do allow the airplane to stop on a soft surface, you may not get it rolling again without assistance. If you should become stuck, don't try to "gun" the airplane out with power while passengers push on struts and wing tips. A misdirected, healthy shove can bend the struts and wing tips, and amid the confusion of engine noise and prop blast, people working around those spinning blades are very likely to get hurt. The safest way is to go for help and bring back boards, a tow bar, and plenty of extra muscle.

As you reach the firmer surface of the tie down area, throttle back to maintain a normal taxi speed.

## The Short Soft Field

If your destination airport is both soft *and* short, you need to ask yourself an important question: "Even if I can get it safely *in*, can I get it safely *out?*" Certainly, if reasoning or common sense suggest that your short-field destination may have a poor surface, a preflight phone call to that field is in order. Tell the airport owner what kind of airplane you'll be flying and get another's thoughts on the matter. And when you arrive, give the runway a low-altitude "fly-by" to decide for yourself. If you have doubts, the solution is simple — *don't land.* Fly to your alternate instead.

If you think the situation is workable and decide to land, put both short-field and soft-field procedures into play, being very careful in case of a go-around. When descending to a short runway in the soft-field configuration (very slow, full flaps, partial power) you must decide early if your glide path is on target. Unless you are experienced at making power-on landings, the unfamiliar power may cause an overshoot; and once the airplane is skimming over the runway, the power may produce unexpected floating. If you have delayed the go-around until this happens, you face two unattractive alternatives: either you must execute a pull-up as your short-field go-around point nears, or you must cut your power to stop floating and land. The go-around in these situations can be hairy. On the one hand you are at an extremely low speed, with full flaps, and very close to the ground. And, on the other, when you cut your power to stop floating, you hit with a high sink rate.

When planning a landing at a short field that has turned soft, the key word is caution. If you have serious doubts as you face the situation, the answer is easy — don't do it.

# IN REVIEW: Soft-Field Operations

### PREFLIGHT REMINDERS

- Use a power-on approach to achieve a low sink rate.
- Use full flaps to allow the slowest safe approach speed.
- Touch down with partial power.
- Roll-out with the stick fully aft and partial power.
- Taxi with partial flaps, partial power, and full back pressure on the stick.
- Evaluate your glide path and decide on any go-around before you reach the runway threshold.

### IN-FLIGHT AIDS

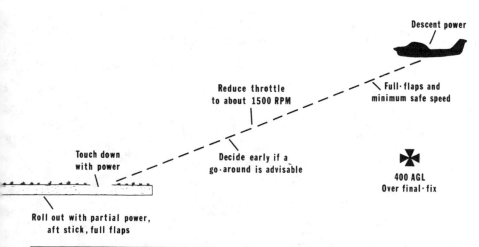

**Fig. 4.3.** The soft-field approach in profile, showing key points at which the pilot takes certain actions.

# 5 | Night Landing Procedures

*Night flight.* The words conjure feelings of pioneering, exploration, adventure. Stars above and ahead seem closer than Earth below, and the pilot's element makes a subtle shift from airspace to simply space.

Minutes are suspended in the darkened cockpit. Dimly glowing instruments hold both time and motion steady. Earthbound clamor cannot penetrate the silence within the engine's rumble. Even fellow pilots aboard seldom disturb the solitude; they too respect the moment. Words are as Spartan as movements, and each are directed toward a purpose. Here you have the chance to think your own thoughts, to consider, for the moment, the reality of *up here* and *down there.*

And the bright planet held centered in the windshield seems a more likely destination than the winking beacon below.

## Basic Considerations

Night landings are not normally hazardous, but they do contain enough uncertainty to keep the touchdown interesting. The basis for these uncertainties lies in three facts. First, many of the landmarks and visual references that help guide us through the landing sequence are simply lost at night. It is difficult to select landmarks to delineate our desired traffic pattern, for example, or pick marks for our final fix, touchdown target, or go-around points. Even the centerline is difficult to see until we are nearly on it.

Second, the lack of daylight produces illusions that can be confusing. Without intermediate and background references, for instance, distance is compressed. What appears to be 5 miles away is really 10. What seems 100 feet is actually 200. Attitudes are easily confused. A line of distant lights at an angle to our approach path, for example, looks like a sloping horizon. It makes one wing appear low and the nose high. Even estimates of time and speed are difficult without visible passage over the ground.

And finally, our eyes just don't see as well at night. The unique construction of our eyes places a nighttime blind spot in our direct line of vision. The best night view comes from the corners of our eyes, and this is difficult to deal with when we are busy with the landing. Insufficient oxygen seriously affects night vision. The pilot descending from cruise altitude has a slight case of hypoxia, as does the pilot in a crowded and stuffy cockpit. Even age plays its part with night vision. It seems that the older we get, the more we have to squint. If you are in my age bracket (between 45 and death), you might even want to invite a younger pair of eyes along on your night flight.

These three facts are behind the uncertainties of night landing. Our choice of airport for a night arrival and our night landing technique must take these basic problems into consideration to render them harmless.

## Selecting an Appropriate Airport

AIRPORT LIGHTING. Whereas a night landing at an unlighted airport is legal, it is seldom safe. It is next to impossible to detect wind drift during the approach to a dark runway. Without a lighted runway, the approaching pilot cannot positively identify the runway threshold or establish a touchdown target. And without a touchdown target, the pilot has little chance of recognizing an overshoot and the need for a go-around until it is too late. Any landing at an unlighted airport should be considered only as an emergency landing.

The minimum airport lighting demanded for safety requires runway edge lights. These are white lights set 200 feet apart that outline the runway. A rotating beacon takes a great deal of strain from the task of locating the airport when flying by night over unfamiliar terrain. If your destination does not have a beacon, make sure that a beaconed airport lies near enough to serve as an alternate. It's no fun to be searching for your night destination with the fuel gauges resting at the quarter mark and with no alternative place to go.

The sectional chart will tell you if runway edge lights or a rotating beacon exist at your destination, but only a preflight briefing from the Flight Service Station tells you whether they are operational. Consult the *Airport/Facility Directory* to determine if the destination airport offers runway end identifier lights or an approach light system. These systems are high-intensity strobes that positively identify the runway threshold or provide runway alignment on final. They are particularly useful when your destination airport lies hidden within the incandescent maze of a large city.

**RUNWAY LENGTH.** The diminished view and the illusions of nighttime landing usually combine to produce an approach that is a trifle high and fast. You are normally unaware of this until you have rounded out and find yourself floating down the runway. Add to this the fact that any selected go-around point can easily pass unnoticed in the dark, and the concern about extra runway length is easy to understand. Apply a rule of thumb: Confine night landings to runways that exceed twice the total-to-clear-obstacle length prescribed by your aircraft handbook.

Runway width must also be considered when planning a night arrival. Last-second puffs of crosswind are extremely difficult to detect at night, and it is very easy to touch down away from the runway's center. Your personal minimum depends on your skill and experience, but most pilots would be wise to choose a runway at least 75 feet wide for nocturnal landings. (Runway width is found in the *Airport/Facility Directory*.)

**RUNWAY SURFACE.** Unless you are either very familiar with the turf field or have considerable night experience, confine your night landings to paved runways. A paved runway (or its strips) reflects illumination from the landing light, making the surface visible during round-out and touchdown. The centerline of the paved runway is invaluable at night for detecting any drift and providing a measure of depth perception. A paved runway's edge is discernible at night, even between the runway lights. This is valuable when you encounter an unexpected swerve during the roll-out.

An unpaved runway, on the other hand, reflects very little light. This, along with the absence of a centerline, makes an accurate touchdown difficult, and it is nearly impossible to detect any drift. A turf runway normally blends right into rough or soft shoulders. Any swerve is likely to continue until the airplane slides to a stop in the rough or the ditch.

**RADAR SERVICES.** If your nighttime destination lies in unfamiliar territory, give some thought to the availability of radar services. You are often tired as you near your destination, and your fuel supply has dwindled. Airports seem to seize this opportunity to hide. And it is then that pilots appreciate the vectoring service of approach control. Radar need not be located at your destination, but should be within 40 miles, which is reasonable radar range. (Availability of radar vectoring is noted in the *Airport/Facility Directory.*)

**ALTERNATE DESTINATION.** If your proposed destination does *not* offer the minimum qualities that you need for a safe night landing, plan alternate action. Fly instead to a nearby airport that *does* meet your qualifications. A short morning flight will put you at your ultimate destination for a daylight landing.

## Night Landing Technique

Keep in mind the three facts that allow uncertainties to creep into the night landing:

1. Many daytime landmarks and visual references are hidden by darkness.
2. Night skies create illusions in attitude, distance, time, and speed.
3. We don't see as well at night as we do during the day.

Incorporate special measures into each step of the landing sequence as you lay plans for a night arrival.

**DESCENDING TO THE DESTINATION AIRPORT.** The same 10- or 20-minute planned descent that works during the day works as well at night. But it is difficult to visually determine just when to start your letdown. The sectional chart and a depicted lighted landmark are needed to determine the required distance. Then confirm this, if possible, with electronic aids: VHF omnirange radial, distance measuring equipment, or a statement of position from a radar controller.

Be sure to jot down the time you begin your descent. This allows you to estimate the midpoint of the letdown. At night, with distance, time, and speed hard to determine visually, you should evaluate your altitude halfway along your descent. This gives you the opportunity to make any readjustments to your rate of descent with the destination still well ahead of you.

Wind drift is difficult to detect during a nighttime descent. You cannot see the drift occurring against the ground, and the wind normally shifts direction at different altitudes. Make use of any available VHF omnirange radial or radar vectoring service if the wind is significant. Knowing the surface wind throughout the descent helps you anticipate any drift as you approach the destination. Even with the airport beacon in sight, an uncorrected wind drift causes you to "home" rather than "track" to the target. You are then apt to be geographically disoriented as you approach the airport at an unexpected heading. You would be wise to check your position against the sectional chart and the lighted landmark when your elapsed time tells you that you are midway through the descent.

Avoiding collisions is a nighttime concern. Traffic is harder to spot, and once seen, it's difficult to determine the distance and direction of travel. Concentrate your defensive flying in two areas: take steps to make your spotting more efficient and make yourself more visible to the other pilots.

Here are a few tips to help improve your chances of seeing the traffic. Remove any items from the top of the instrument panel and dim the cockpit lights to minimize distracting reflections from the windshield and windows. If you're descending from an altitude of even 5000 or 6000 feet, your vision is slightly impaired from the reduced oxygen. If you have supplemental oxygen aboard, a whiff brightens the night. Likewise, a crowded and stuffy cockpit is low in oxygen; open the vents for a faceful of fresh air. Also, a stuffy cockpit on a cool night may call for a terrycloth wipedown of the windows. Cease unnecessary cockpit conversation and assign each passenger a sector of the sky to guard. Most passengers are more than willing, and without a busy airplane to fly, they are usually effective at the job. As you search for traffic, let your eyes do as much of the scanning as possible. Minimize head movement, both for an unblurred view and to reduce the chance of vertigo. Even your ears help spot traffic if you maintain a listening watch on the arrival frequency. Just remember to listen for departing traffic as well as the position reports of inbound planes.

Use radar traffic advisory services anytime it is available. Doing so not only gives you another pair of eyes to help look for traffic but also helps the other participating pilots spot you. Accurate position reporting, whether to approach control, tower, or unicom, helps other pilots spot your plane. As a final defensive measure, turn on your landing light at the midpoint of your letdown. Traffic gets heavier as you near the airport, and the hardest airplane to spot is the one directly ahead and traveling toward you. Head-on traffic presents little relative movement, and if an airplane is climbing toward you, it is hidden by your airplane's nose. But with your landing light blazing away, the other pilot cannot miss seeing you. And as long as *one pilot sees,* there is no collision.

If your destination airport rests within a city, locate the beacon and fix its position in your mind while you are still several miles out, for it will surely disappear into the blaze of city lights as the town draws near. Visualize the lay of the active runway with your heading indicator and use your sectional chart to select the 5-mile landmark for your 45-degree approach to the downwind leg of the traffic pattern.

**ENTERING THE TRAFFIC PATTERN.** Night flying requires extra time to interpret and act. We take a second look to satisfy ourselves that we see what we see. And we're constantly taking the time to scan our instruments to confirm altitude, heading, airspeed, and attitude. Compensate for this "cockpit slowdown" by slowing your airplane to pattern speed before you enter the downwind. If you are flying a retractable-gear airplane, have the gear down and locked prior to entering the pattern.

Identify the runway lights as you approach the pattern, then pick parallel lighted points to mark the downwind leg. Finding those runway lights at a big city airport is often a challenge; they blend into the city lights. Usually, however, the tower operator can increase the intensity of the runway edge lights and is glad to do so at the pilot's request. You can then easily find the runway.

**FLYING THE TRAFFIC PATTERN.** Even with lighted landmarks, wind drift is hard to detect when flying a nighttime pattern. Take note of the runway's relative position to your wing tip when you establish your pattern. Your relative position should remain fairly constant throughout the downwind and base legs, and any discrepancy in the "gap" between wing tip and runway serves as an indication of drift. Your best defense against undetected drift, however, is awareness of the wind. Know the wind's direction before you enter the pattern and anticipate the correction you need on each pattern leg.

As you fly the downwind leg, select lighted landmarks for your half-mile final-fix point, touchdown target, and go-around point. Estimate the half-mile fix against the known lighted runway length. Select the third set of runway edge lights as your touchdown target; runway lights are placed 200 feet apart. Plan a go-around point that leaves at least six sets of runway lights ahead as you touch down. Some light airplanes may require more stopping distance. Check your aircraft manual if in doubt.

Positively identify the threshold before you turn base leg, and keep it in sight (along with your final-fix point) throughout your descent on downwind and base legs. If you do not have it in sight before turning base, you stand little chance of spotting it while you are busy managing the descent. By the same token, if you lose sight of the threshold during the descending turns to the runway, your position in the letdown will be in doubt. And flying a few hundred feet above the ground at night is no place for doubts.

**DESCENDING TO THE RUNWAY.** The daytime 400 feet AGL over the final-fix point works well at night, but you have to depend more on your altimeter than during daylight to achieve it. Even with a reevaluation of your glide path every 50 feet, you are likely to overshoot or undershoot the final-fix point. Without the visual clue of the ground coming closer, an accurate descent is difficult to achieve. If you reach 400 feet AGL prior to your final fix, increase your throttle to the power required to hold altitude at approach speed. Then reduce the throttle again as you cross the fix. If, on the other hand, you cross the fix with excess altitude, start an early power reduction as you head toward the runway.

Once established on final, concentrate on your touchdown target — those third runway lights. You will be able to detect any apparent motion of your target, even at night. If it is apparent that you are significantly overshooting or undershooting, opt for an early go-around. Delaying any go-around until the last moment imposes considerable risk on a night landing. It is easy to float right past the go-around point without seeing it. Once a night go-around commences, pitch and airspeed are difficult to interpret against a featureless background.

Cross the threshold at a minimum of 100 feet AGL and make a brief check of airspeed, runway alignment, and the projected glide path relative to your touchdown target and well short of the go-around point that leaves six runway lights ahead as the tires touch.

**ROUNDING OUT.** It is next to impossible to accurately gauge those last few feet of altitude at night. As you round out, smoothly establish a touchdown attitude that has the nose just covering the last set of runway lights at the far end. Then hold that attitude, slowly reduce any power remaining, and let the runway come up to meet the tires. Stretch your neck to keep the centerline in sight as long as possible to detect any last-second wind drift. When your vision directly over the nose is finally blocked, shift your line of sight slightly left, alongside the nose, to monitor the runway edge and the approaching go-around point.

**TOUCHING DOWN.** The nighttime touchdown usually comes as a mild surprise; you can't tell exactly when to expect it. Do not, however, let the surprise trigger a yank on the stick. When the tires touch, *slowly* bring the stick back. If the airplane should take a small bounce, just continue to hold the stick back and apply crosswind correction. Normally the airplane takes two more bounces, then settles down. A large bounce, of course, calls for a bit of power to soften the ensuing touchdown or, possibly, calls for a go-around.

**ROLLING OUT.** Keep your eyes locked on the space between the last lights at the runway's end. If you let your eyes stray for even a moment at night, you are likely to swerve. The close proximity of the centerline stripes flashing through the patch of landing light and the runway lights zipping past the wing tips give the illusion of excess roll-out speed. Curb any urge for excess braking and bring the plane to a stop astride the centerline.

**CLEARING THE RUNWAY.** Taxi down the runway centerline until you positively identify the runway exit. When you find the taxiway, stop momentarily in midrunway and take a close look around the exit before you approach it. Look for airplanes that are either holding or taxiing toward your runway for an intersection takeoff.

**TAXIING TO THE RAMP.** Follow three cardinal rules when you taxi at night: taxi slowly, taxi only with your taxi or landing light on, and taxi only on designated taxiways or taxi areas. Your viewing range is limited to artificial light at night, and obstacles and moving vehicles can leap out of nowhere. Sudden stops are commonplace, and these are possible only with a slow taxi speed.

Keep your taxi or landing light operating anytime your airplane is moving. Taxiing an airplane through darkness without lights is no safer than driving a car at night with no lights.

Taxiways are designated by a yellow centerline and/or blue edge lights. Taxi areas are designated taxi routes across large paved areas and are delineated by a yellow centerline and double yellow edge stripes. Taxiways and taxi areas are maintained for safe travel. Any nondesignated area may contain hazards that a taxi light cannot pick up in time for pilot action.

When you taxi at night, devote your full attention to the task at hand. Keep your vision directed outside the cockpit any time the airplane is moving. If a task inside the cockpit demands your attention, stop the airplane while you attend to it. Remember that pilots hit things at night simply because they either are not looking or the darkness will not let them see in time.

**SHUTTING DOWN.** Avoid parking in close quarters at night. It's hard to tell just how much distance remains between the wing tip and the obstacle, and whacking a hangar wall with the wing makes a bang that echoes in a pilot's memory for months. At night it is far better to shut down in an open area and then hand-move the plane into the close tiedown space, with an assistant keeping tabs on the wing tips and tail (Fig. 5.1).

Give your passengers detailed instructions on deplaning. Handholds, step areas, and foot spuds are hard to find at night unless you are familiar with the airplane. And if you are flying a high-wing airplane, be sure to mention how old pilots get those creases on the tops of their heads from the trailing edge. Deplaning passengers tend to do the unexpected at night. I think I shall never forget the passenger who climbed out of the Mooney cockpit onto the wing and clomped the full 16-foot length of that convenient aluminum walkway.

**Fig. 5.1.** At night, shut down in an open area. Then hand-move the plane into its close tiedown space.

## Preflight Reminders

Federal Aviation Regulations specify pilots must have a degree of recent night experience if passengers are aboard. FAR 61.57 requires you to make and log three night landings within the preceding 90 days in an airplane of the same category and class as the one you intend to use. But is this legal minimum adequate for safe flight? In most cases, probably not. Night landings are demanding. They require special techniques and considerations, and a busy cockpit a few hundred feet above the ground is no place for you to start remembering the special problems involved. If you have had little night experience within the preceding few weeks, get an hour of intensive dual night instruction, including no-light landings, before you embark into the nighttime sky as pilot in command.

It is important to be thoroughly familiar with the airplane you fly at night, particularly its rate of sink and the cockpit layout. Depth perception is poor during the descent to the runway and the round-out, and you must have a good idea of the way the airplane settles. Your manipulation of the controls and switches must become second nature at night. Your attention is taken up with the landing itself, and you simply do not have time to search out a needed knob, handle, or switch in the darkened cockpit. Know where to reach without looking.

**PERSONAL EQUIPMENT.** Always have a flashlight and sectional chart immediately at hand when flying at night. Instrument lights fail, and charts and tables are hard to read in dim cockpit lighting. I've found small disposable penlights to be very useful. They are small enough to fit handily in a shirt pocket, and are easy to hold while you fly. (They are even easy to hold in your mouth if you need both hands free.) Their small spot of light is adequate for map and instrument reading, but does not reduce your night vision.

Have a sectional chart at hand even on local flights. Things just *look* different at night, and you can get lost in your own backyard. If your proposed flight path comes within a half-hour's cruising range of the chart's edge, have the adjacent chart too.

**INSTRUMENT REFERENCE CAPABILITY.** With so many of the outside visual references lost and with the night's illusions, at least a minimum degree of instrument proficiency is needed for safe night landings. Give yourself this simple instrument flight test the next time you have an observer pilot and a hood aboard: First, establish the airplane in slow flight at approach speed, then put on the hood and make a descending turn to a reciprocal heading and level out 1000 feet below your initial altitude.

Unless you held your airspeed within 10 MPH or your roll-out within 20 degrees of the reciprocal heading, or you leveled off within 100 feet of the desired altitude, you need to tone up your instrument capability before flying at night.

## IN REVIEW: Night Landing Procedures

PREFLIGHT REMINDERS

- Night landings include three sources of difficulty:
    1. Landmarks are not visible.
    2. The lack of daylight produces illusions.
    3. We simply do not see as well at night as we do by day.
- Factors to consider when selecting a nighttime airport:
    1. Airport lighting.
    2. Runway length and width.
    3. Runway surface.
    4. Availability of radar service.
    5. Appropriate alternate airport.
- Descending from cruise altitude to the airport:
    1. Confirm your distance from the airport with electronic navigational aids.
    2. Note the time you begin your descent to help estimate the midpoint of the letdown.
    3. Evaluate your rate of descent midway through the letdown.
    4. Remain aware of the surface wind direction and velocity throughout the descent to the airport.
    5. Descend with the landing light on to make your airplane visible.
    6. Use visual flight rules radar traffic advisories to help spot night traffic.
- Entering the traffic pattern at night:
    1. Enter with a slow airspeed.
    2. Positively identify the runway lights.

- Flying the night traffic pattern:
  1. Remain alert for wind drift.
  2. Positively identify the threshold before you turn base leg.
- Descending to the runway:
  1. Greater dependence on the altimeter is needed at night to arrive over the final-fix point at 400 feet AGL.
  2. Use the third set of runway lights as a touchdown target.
  3. Respond to any apparent overshoot or undershoot with an early go-around.
- Rounding out:
  1. It is almost impossible to predict exactly when the tires will touch.
  2. Let the airplane settle to the runway in a touchdown attitude.
- Touching down:
  1. Do not let the touchdown trigger a yank on the stick.
  2. If the airplane bounces, maintain your crosswind correction.
- Rolling out:
  1. Nighttime roll-outs have the illusion of excessive speed.
  2. Keep your eyes straight ahead while the airplane is rolling.
- Clearing the runway:
  1. Carefully check the runway exit for other airplanes before you leave the runway.
- Taxiing to the ramp at night:
  1. Taxi slowly.
  2. Taxi with the landing light on.
  3. Taxi only on designated taxiways.
- Shutting down:
  1. Avoid parking in close quarters at night.
  2. Give your passengers detailed instructions on deplaning.
- Federal Aviation Regulations specify a degree of recent flight experience.

- Know your airplane thoroughly:
  1. Cockpit and panel layout.
  2. Sink rate.
- Personal equipment:
  1. Flashlight.
  2. Sectional chart.
- A minimum degree of instrument proficiency is needed for safe night approaches and landings.

IN-FLIGHT AIDS

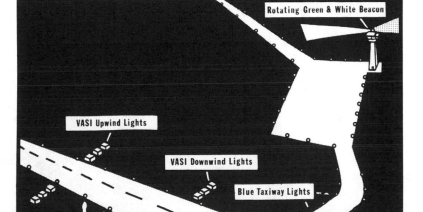

**Fig. 5.2.** Basic airport lighting.

# 6 | Emergency Landings

AN EMERGENCY LANDING comes in one of two forms. We normally picture the forced emergency landing — the sudden loss of power, for example, or the in-flight fire that means the airplane is going down *now*. In the impending emergency landing, on the other hand, you know you will *soon* face an emergency landing. An unsafe gear indication or insufficient fuel to reach an airport are typical instances.

The chance that a particular pilot will ever experience an emergency landing is remote, but we know that it can happen. It can even happen to us. And once can be too often if you do not respond correctly to the situation. While it is certainly nothing to look forward to, the emergency landing can be handled with a degree of safety if you act quickly and correctly.

Pilots come to grief in emergency landings for a twofold reason. They go through their flying careers feeling that an emergency landing will never face them, so they never formulate a plan of action against the occurrence. Then, when it does happen, they are unwilling and unprepared to accept it. They delay taking action; they feel that the situation is beyond their control, that fate is in command. And, finally, with the uprushing ground a hard and unmistakable reality, they act out a frantic chain of mistakes that carries them right down to impact.

If you have not already formulated your own emergency landing procedure, do so now, keeping in mind three factors (Fig. 6.1):

1. Your plan must work in a variety of emergency landing situations.
2. Your plan must be kept simple.
3. Your plan must allow for misjudgments.

> 1. WILL WORK IN A VARIETY OF SITUATIONS
> 2. SIMPLE TO EXECUTE
> 3. ALLOWS FOR MISJUDGEMENTS

**Fig. 6.1.** An emergency procedure must include three basic factors.

We cannot anticipate the exact circumstances of an emergency landing. There are just too many variables — terrain, wind, cruising altitude, visibility, to name a few. Our contingency plan, therefore, must adequately (if not perfectly) fit the particular set of circumstances we face. Let's make plans for three categories of emergency landings: the forced landing from cruising altitude, the forced landing following takeoffs, and the impending emergency landing for which the pilot has time to plan careful steps.

Keep your emergency procedure simple. Remember, this is the sort of plan that you keep filed in the back of your mind for years and hope you never have to use. But if you should need to pull the plan of action out of the file, it must be simple enough to recall (Fig. 6.2).

---

**Fig. 6.2.** A pilot rarely becomes an expert at emergency landings but is usually engaging in on-the-job training when one comes along. So keep your contingency plans simple.

Pilots do not become experts at making emergency landings; they are usually blazing a new trail for themselves when one comes along. Add to this the fact that emergency circumstances provide ample opportunity for making mistakes, and we quickly see why plans must anticipate misjudgments and render them as harmless as possible.

## Forced Landing from Cruising Altitude

A forced landing from cruise flight announces itself in very certain terms. One moment you are flying contentedly, the passengers are talking among themselves, and steady RPMs sing their song of flight. Then — a sputter, and engine and passengers go quiet. The tachometer seems to have a will of its own, and suddenly you are no longer content.

If you took an instant to look over your right shoulder, you would see all eyes fixed on *you*. You would know that in the next few minutes you must deliver the finest piece of piloting you have ever flown. React. First, take a split second to remind yourself that even though the engine may be dead, the rest of the airplane certainly isn't. Ailerons, rudder, and elevator still respond to your command, and you are still very much a pilot. Second, order your passengers (and yourself), "Stay calm! Keep still!" Panic in the cockpit is more than any pilot should have to bear when handling an emergency aloft, and most passengers will behave if the pilot simply asks them to. And, finally, put into play a six-step procedure formulated around the basic considerations of a forced landing from cruise flight (Fig. 6.3):

1. Establish the best glide speed.
2. Select a landing area.
3. Fly toward the landing area.
4. Try a restart/communicate/prepare for the landing.
5. Fly a simple square approach pattern and land.
6. Evacuate the airplane.

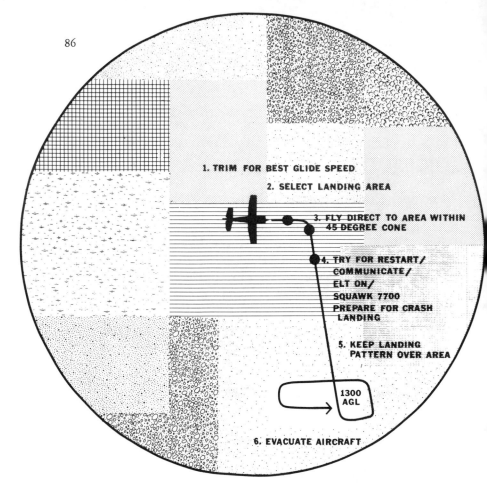

1. TRIM FOR BEST GLIDE SPEED

2. SELECT LANDING AREA

3. FLY DIRECT TO AREA WITHIN 45 DEGREE CONE

4. TRY FOR RESTART/ COMMUNICATE/ ELT ON/ SQUAWK 7700 PREPARE FOR CRASH LANDING

5. KEEP LANDING PATTERN OVER AREA

1300 AGL

6. EVACUATE AIRCRAFT

**Fig. 6.3.** Put into play a six-step procedure formulated around the basic considerations of a forced landing from cruise flight.

**ESTABLISH THE BEST GLIDE SPEED.** Quickly establish the speed that gives the maximum glide range and, just as important, trim for that airspeed. Then, if the tensions and distractions of the situation cause you to temporarily neglect precise flying, the airplane will continue to do its best to give you maximum distance.

The airplane's best glide airspeed is given in the aircraft handbook. But if you do not know it, don't take time to look it up while you're losing altitude. Instead, use this rule of thumb: In a fixed-gear aircraft, use a glide speed one-third greater than the lowest figure in the airspeed indicator's green arc. In a retract-able-gear aircraft, increase the minimum green arc speed by 50 percent. These speeds very nearly match the handbook's best glide airspeed.

**SELECT A LANDING AREA.** After setting the airplane's best glide speed, find a place to land. Remember to look out both sides of the cockpit; there is a strong tendency to search only to the left, out the nearest window. To minimize the need for experience and judgment, select a spot that lies within a 45-degree cone; that is, picture your airplane at the top of a cone that has sides slanting in a 45-degree angle down to the ground (Fig. 6.4). Then look

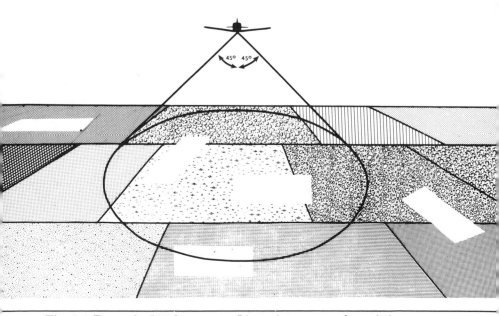

**Fig. 6.4.** To use the "45-degree cone," just picture your plane sitting on a cone that has sides slanting 45 degrees down to the ground.

down the 45-degree angle and pick a spot that lies inside the cone's base. By confining your landing area to this cone, you are assured of reaching it, even against a moderate wind, toward upsloping terrain, or with a poorly flown airplane. Most light airplanes glide about 2 miles for every 1000 feet of altitude when properly flown and with no wind. But even a well-pitched horseshoe can make good a 45-degree glide path.

Choose the largest open area within your 45-degree cone that is free of obviously dangerous obstacles. Don't try to analyze the texture of the surface closely. If it looks reasonable and the area is big enough, go for it. Often you may try to outglide your experience and the airplane's capability because you are overly concerned with preventing damage to the airplane. You overreach the glide path in an attempt to reach an ideal landing surface. It is far better to concern yourself with preventing serious injury to yourself and your passengers; go for the nearest, "reasonable" landing area rather than gamble on the distant ideal.

**FLY TOWARD THE LANDING AREA.** Once you have picked your landing area, fly directly to it, still conserving altitude with best glide airspeed. Do not maneuver for landing position or eliminate any excess altitude until you are over your field. Any attempt to S-turn or otherwise position your airplane for an approach while en route to your field depends on experience and judgment. And any misjudgment could land you short of your target. Plan instead to do any maneuvering directly over the field when you reach it.

Once you have selected your field and turned toward it, never take your eyes from it. If you look inside the cockpit and inadvertently let the airplane turn while doing so, you may be unable to relocate your landing area. Resist the temptation to exchange your selected field for a better-looking one that lies just a little further on. Unless a change of fields is unavoidable, stick to your original plan. Should you need to pick another area, just make sure it lies within your 45-degree cone.

**TRY A RESTART/CALL FOR HELP/PREPARE FOR THE LANDING.**
If altitude permits any extra time while you head for your landing area, put those minutes to work. First, try to get the engine
running again. Check the two most common causes of sudden
engine failure — fuel starvation and lack of ignition. Pull the
carburetor heat, switch tanks, turn on the boost pump, push the
mixture to rich, and try each magneto in turn.

If the engine doesn't restart and time remains, put out a call
for help. Squawk 7700 on your transponder and transmit a Mayday call on 121.5. Most Federal Aviation Administration (FFA)
towers, flight service stations, and radar facilities monitor the
121.5 emergency frequency, and your broadcast reaches out 60
miles from even 2000 feet. Include eight items in your Mayday call:

1. "Mayday, Mayday, Mayday."
2. Aircraft identification.
3. Type of aircraft and color.
4. Advise that you're making a forced landing.
5. Number of people aboard.
6. Position.
7. Request for help.
8. Activate the emergency locator transmitter.

In an emergency, passengers are usually willing to help the
pilot if asked. If time remains, assign jobs to each passenger to
prepare for landing. Give a passenger the responsibility for
checking seat belts and harnesses and collecting any padding
available for head protection. A cabin cleanup to collect all hard,
loose objects and stow them on the rear floor can be handled by
another passenger. And assign the front seat passenger the task
of unlatching the door as the landing approach commences. This,
of course, prevents a hard landing from jamming the door closed.

**FLY AN EMERGENCY APPROACH PATTERN AND LAND.** Once over
your landing area, spiral away any excess altitude while still
maintaining best glide speed and remaining within the confines of

the area. Maintaining the best glide descent allows you maximum time to plan your approach and landing. By remaining within the boundaries of your landing area, there is little chance for any misjudgment to carry you beyond gliding range.

As you begin to spiral over the area, decide on the landing direction and roll-out path. Try to prevent an approach over obstacles or a roll-out that aims your airplane at a solid obstruction. Once you have chosen your "runway," pick a spot at its midpoint to serve as your touchdown target, rather than a point near the approach end of your landing strip. Again, you are protecting against misjudgment. If you plan to touch down at the near end of your landing area and you misjudge short, you could be in trouble. But if you plan for the midpoint, you've given yourself margin for error.

When your spiral brings you to 1300 feet AGL (the number 13 should be easy to remember in a forced landing), move to the downwind leg. Fly a familiar square pattern, but keep it within one-half mile of your touchdown target. Plan to turn final at 500 feet AGL, but if you reach 500 feet AGL while still on base leg, turn toward your touchdown target at that time.

When you see that you have your target definitely made, lower a notch of flaps and your landing gear. When you reach the near edge of the landing area, extend full flaps to land short of your midpoint target. Once your gear and flaps are down, turn off the master switch, ignition, and fuel flow to lessen the chance of fire.

Expect a number of distractions when you hit. It will not be a smooth touchdown. The plane will shake, rattle, and bang like a barrel riding over the falls; two buckets of dust and dirt will sift out of nowhere; and the passengers will probably release their pent-up opinions. Rudder pedals will try to bounce away from your feet as the nosewheel rolls over ruts and ridges. But you must stay on them to steer clear of any head-on obstacles. Brake the airplane to a stop as soon as possible.

**EVACUATE THE AIRPLANE.** Your main concern now is fire. It can happen quickly, and split seconds count. Tell your passengers to get out and move well away from the airplane. Don't allow any of them time to locate any baggage or personal items. See that they are all moving, then get out and take the passengers 50 yards away from the airplane and don't approach it again for 20 minutes.

File a plan of action in your mind. Then, when a forced landing from altitude faces you, carry out that plan; you have a better than reasonable chance of coming through with no serious injury to your passengers or yourself.

## The Forced Landing Following Takeoff

A pilot who loses an engine shortly after liftoff, with the airport already behind, faces a truly desperate situation. Survival is in question. There is time for only the most meager of discrepancy checks; switch tanks and verify that the ignition is on "both." Then the critical question — turn back to the airport or seek another landing area? The answer is rarely clear-cut. There are few hard-and-fast rules for guidance because the circumstances are so varied and there are so few pilots with personal experience to pass along first-hand knowledge. Here, however, are some basic concepts for you to consider to improve your chances if faced with a forced landing right after takeoff. (Notice that I ask you to *consider* rather than to do. I certainly am not experienced at making forced landings. I have, however, conducted many simulated forced landings with pilots of all skill levels. I endeavor to keep the simulations as realistic as possible, and my insights and comments are based on these enactments. But there is a void between realistic and real. How narrow or how wide that void is, I cannot say with certainty. Therefore, regard the comments as circumstantial evidence. Weigh them against your own logic, and, if the ideas make sense, adopt them as your own.)

KNOW YOUR AIRPORT. If a forced landing from takeoff should ever come your way, the chances are that it will happen from the airport you use most — your home field. Spend some time in a closed circuit, touch-and-go pattern to survey the departure paths for acceptable emergency landing areas. With each arrival and departure thereafter, a check on the current status of your selections serves to implant them into reflex memory should the need arise. Conduct a similar survey of the airports that you frequently visit, and you have eliminated a significant measure of uncertainty from a forced landing.

While on arrival to an unfamiliar airport, remember that you will also soon depart that airport. So on the downwind leg, look at the departure path of the runway and spot a likely emergency landing area. Then, should power fail when a turn back to the field is inadvisable, you have an idea where relative safety lies.

**KNOW YOUR AIRPLANE.** When do I have enough altitude to turn back, and when must I land ahead? The answer to this question lies in your knowledge of your airplane. And you can gain that knowledge only through practical experience.

Let's set up three rules of thumb and then modify them somewhat for the plane you fly.

1. If the engine fails at 1000 feet AGL and the airport boundary lies no more than one-half mile behind, execute a 180-degree return to the field.
2. If the engine fails at 500 feet AGL, select an emergency area that lies within a half-mile glide and 90 degrees of turn.
3. If the engine fails below 500 feet, select the best area within a quarter-mile glide and 30 degrees of turn.

To modify these rules of thumb for the airplane you fly, practice three exercises that place you and your machine in corresponding simulated situations. With an observer pilot aboard to help spot planes, fly to an airport that offers a long paved runway and little traffic.

*Exercise 1.* Overfly the runway at 1000 feet AGL and at a slow-flight speed that approximates climb airspeed. Begin your simulated forced landing one-half mile beyond the airport boundary. Close the throttle, taking the time (simulating emergency actions) to confirm the altitude, and touch the fuel selector handle and ignition switch. Then turn back to the airport, establish best glide speed, and decide whether you could glide safely to the unobstructed airport area for an emergency landing. You may be surprised at the amount of altitude that the turns cost you, and this lack of knowledge has led many pilots to serious injury. Expect the downwind approach to produce a shallow glide and excess ground speed.

Modify through trial and error the gliding distance of rule one to match the capabilities of plane and pilot. But be careful that your modified rule does not risk overreaching that capability. Pilots who attempt to turn back with insufficient altitude for the distance run the risk of either hitting the ground while still in a turn or trying to stretch the glide. Either produces disaster. If a plane is turning when it hits, it is very likely to catch a wing tip and cartwheel. The pilot and passengers probably would not survive. In attempting to stretch the glide (which really shortens the glide), the pilot becomes intent on making the field and is then in great danger of stalling the airplane. Again, if an airplane stalls and falls that last 50 feet, survival is doubtful.

*Exercise 2*. Approach the runway in slow flight at 90 degrees, one-half mile out, and at 500 feet AGL. Then, with the airplane in position, begin the exercise. Close the throttle, simulate the brief discrepancy check, and turn toward the runway. Gauge the airplane's capability against the figures of rule 2. And again, through experiment, modify the rule for your airplane.

*Exercise 3*. Approach the runway threshold at a 30-degree angle. Have the plane slowed to simulate climb speed and descend so that you reach the airport boundary 200 feet AGL. Then, as the threshold nears, close your throttle and make the shallow turn toward the landing. You will discover that even a shallow turn costs altitude. Evaluate the distance required and make any needed modifications to rule 3.

Will your three rules of thumb provide the perfect solution for the actual forced landing that you could someday encounter shortly after takeoff? Probably not. There are just too many variables. But, as you develop your rules, you see what your airplane is capable of achieving in three representative situations. Keep these tentative plans filed in your memory as a visualized action based on your own observation and personal experience. And should the occasion arise, you have in a sense "been there." Your memory has a good chance to trigger a workable solution.

IF NO LANDING AREA EXISTS. Even the big city airport usually offers a possible nearby landing area — a body of water, a park, an expressway median. But ocasionally there is nothing. Circumstances may leave you no way out. And then you must land where you cannot land.

If you are totally frightened and your fright rings the alarm of finality, you experience two reactions. First, the adrenalin does not surge; you are beyond that point. Second, you try very hard not to make a mistake. For me, a forced landing from takeoff with no landable patch of survival in sight would be such an occasion. Logic tells me that chances favor severe injury. Yet I also know that I could still control the airplane and the crash to a degree. And if ever confronted with the nightmare, I would use that control to reach the ground in a landing attitude and at the lowest possible approach speed, while avoiding a head-on collision with anything solid.

Picture yourself in this situation: your engine quit seconds ago at 400 feet AGL, with the airport well behind and nothing but a busy midmorning city beneath. You've turned toward the only opening you could find — a wide street in a business area. Now, at 100 feet and lined up with the street, you easily see the lamp posts bordering your landing area, the power lines stretched across each corner, delivery vans, cars, people. You hold a straight approach path with ailerons and rudder, vaguely realizing that you're gripping the wheel with both hands, elbows locked straight. A rear seat passenger is trying to say something, but it might as well be in a foreign tongue; your entire concentration is straight ahead. On either side, walls of brick, cement, and windows rise above you, the windmilling prop cuts through the first web of power lines with a blue flash, and your airplane's nose is down in an attempt to maintain approach speed. Below are people, some frozen looking up, some running, others unaware of what is about to happen. You're aware that all the passengers are moving now, shouting. You lift the nose for the round-out and an oncoming Chevrolet jumps the curb, more power lines pass overhead, and your projected descent path points to an intersection filled with a steady flow of traffic crossing on the green.

It is at this point of crisis that you must try your very hardest. You cannot give up; you must keep working and thinking right up to the last moment, and even into that moment. Because that last instant of aircraft control could very well be the deciding factor.

Of course, there can be a bigger question at stake: The welfare of the occupants versus the welfare of those on the ground. But this is a question that can be answered only if, and when, a pilot ever comes face to face with the unavoidable decision.

## The Impending Emergency Landing

Anytime the airplane you are flying suddenly *smells* different (like a whiff of hydraulic fluid for example), *feels* different (like rudder pedals that push unevenly), *sounds* different (like something is fluttering in the wind), or *looks* different (like an instrument needle is pointing where it shouldn't) — one thing is certain; the airplane *is* different. And that difference could be an in-flight discrepancy that gives you early warning of an impending emergency landing. When your senses suggest that something is different, begin an immediate investigation. (I've not yet felt compelled to *taste* an airplane, but I'm not through flying yet, either.)

If your investigation indicates an in-flight problem, pinpoint the discrepancy, try to determine its cause, and attempt to remedy it. If, for example, the oil temperature needle is someplace you've never seen it before — long past the E, going through M, and headed for the P — look for the cause. An abnormally high outside air temperature could be at fault or a combination of high power and lean mixture, a prolonged climb, or an internal engine malfunction. Take remedial action. Open the cowl flaps, for instance, enrich the mixture, or reduce power.

The aircraft handbook or flight manual usually outlines steps for remedying the more common in-flight discrepancies. And if you would like outside help, call it in. A call on Unicom can normally put you in touch with a mechanic that knows your airplane's systems. Very few discrepancies are unique, and the chances are good that an experienced mechanic will recognize the symptoms you describe and have the solution. A mechanic may be able to help you determine, for example, whether you have a faulty gear extension or only a faulty warning indicator — or advise you exactly how low the oil pressure can drop before the engine seizes up. If the mechanic doesn't seem to have the answers, don't hesitate to call elsewhere for a second opinion.

If you are unable to remedy the in-flight discrepancy and harbor any doubts about the safety of continuing on to the destination — don't. Instead, begin preparations for an impending emergency landing by executing three preliminary steps:

1. Determine the time you can remain aloft.
2. Select an adequate airport.
3. Communicate with the nearest Flight Service Station (FSS) or Air Traffic Control (ATC) facility.

Gauge the flying time you have left against the total situation; check fuel remaining, weather conditions, approaching darkness, and the nature of the discrepancy itself. Plan to have the airplane on the ground and the emergency behind you with a reserve of fuel aboard, even if your discrepancy *is* low fuel and your ability to reach an airport is in doubt. It is far better to select an emergency landing area and land under power than to have one forced on you, where you must land with a dead engine because you tried vainly to reach an airport. Worsening weather conditions shorten the time aloft for dealing with an emergency. Lowering clouds, for example, cancel your best insurance — altitude. Reduced visibility complicates navigation and makes traffic spotting additionally difficult for an already distracted pilot. Similarly, try to plan your impending emergency landing before darkness catches you. The nature of the discrepancy may impose its own time limit. A rough engine, for example, usually runs a long time, but if the oil pressure is dropping, your time aloft is limited.

In general, a paved airport is easier to locate than an unpaved airport. Paved runways stand out against the terrain, whereas turf strips have had years of practice at hiding from pilots who have a desperate need to "get it on the ground." If you are over unfamiliar territory and face this choice, consider navigating to the more distant paved airport rather than to the nearer sod field.

Take time to consider the service facilities needed to meet your airplane's discrepancy. At the very least, you probably will want a repair shop. If you anticipate the possibility of aircraft damage or injury, such as gear-up landing, you would be wise to select a large city airport with competent fire and rescue equipment. And don't hesitate to ask that they be standing by. If, however, the nature of your difficulty holds the prospect of a sudden forced landing, (low oil pressure, low fuel, a progressively worsening engine) you may want to select a rural airport surrounded by unpopulated landing areas. Flight Service is an invaluable source of information when selecting an airport adequate for your emergency landing.

After you have evaluated the seriousness of your problem, estimated how long you can stay in the air, and decided on an airport, radio the nearest FSS or ATC facility. Let them know that you have trouble aboard and may later need to declare an emergency. The FSS personnel and ATC controllers cannot make decisions for the pilot in distress, nor can they fly the airplane. You must rely on your own knowledge, skill, and judgment to see your airplane and passengers through the difficulty. But at the pilot's request, ground support can offer information for you to act upon and can render services that ease your work load. Unfortunately, it often happens that pilots delay calls for assistance until the emergency is actually at hand. By that time options are usually so limited that information or service is of little value.

After you make contact with the ground facility and they know your problem, consider requesting any or all of the following:

1. A radar or direction finder (DF) confirmation of your present location.
2. An updated weather briefing.
3. Radar vectors or DF steers to the alternate airport.
4. Visual flight rules radar traffic advisories.
5. A confirmation of your estimated time of arrival.
6. Alerting the alternate airport of your difficulty.

Formulate your own procedure to meet the forced landing from cruise altitude, the forced landing following takeoff and the impending forced landing. After you have designed your procedures, test them in practical simulations. Then, every 24 months thereafter, give yourself a rehearsal just prior to participating in your biennial flight review, and ask your reviewer to put your procedures to the test.

---

1. ESTABLISH BEST GLIDE SPEED.
2. SELECT A LANDING AREA.
3. FLY DIRECT TO LANDING AREA.
4. TRY FOR A RESTART/COMMUNICATE/ PREPARE FOR LANDING.
5. FLY A SIMPLE SQUARE PATTERN AND LAND.
6. EVACUATE THE AIRCRAFT.

**Fig. 6.5.** Emergency landing checklist.

# IN REVIEW: Emergency Landings

### PREFLIGHT REMINDERS

- Plan and practice procedures for:
  1. Forced emergency landings from cruise altitude.
  2. Forced emergency landings following takeoff.
  3. Impending emergency landings.
- Plan your emergency procedures to include three factors:
  1. The plan of action must work in a variety of situations.
  2. The plan must be simple.
  3. The plan must allow for misjudgments.

# In-Flight Guides — for Practicing Emergency Procedures

CHECKLIST: Forced Landing from Cruise Altitude (Fig. 6.5):

- Establish best glide speed:
  1. Airspeed, _____ knots.
  2. Trim for the airspeed.
- Select a landing area:
  1. Within 45-degree cone.
  2. Choose largest open field with reasonable surface.
- Fly toward the landing area:
  1. Fly direct route; don't maneuver for position.
  2. Conserve altitude with best glide speed.
  3. Keep the area in constant view.
  4. Resist the urge to switch fields.
- If time permits — try for a restart/communicate/prepare for a crash landing/activate the emergency locater transmitter
  1. Pull carburetor heat, switch tanks, turn on boost pump, richen mixture, check magnetos.
  2. Squawk 7700, transmit 121.5.
  3. Check all seat belts and harnesses.
  4. Have passengers gather all loose objects; use padding for head protection.

- Fly an emergency approach pattern and land.
  1. Keep all maneuvering within the boundary of the landing area.
  2. Try to select an approach path without obstacles.
  3. Begin a square pattern at 1300 feet AGL.
  4. Aim for the area's midpoint.
- Evacuate the airplane:
  1. Do so without delay.
  2. Greatest hazard is fire — it happens quickly.

(Note: When practicing simulated forced landings, clear the engine frequently, do not descend below 500 feet AGL, and guard against carburetor ice.)

---

WORKSHEET: Forced Landing Following Takeoff

- If the engine fails at 1000 feet AGL and the airport boundary lies no more than _____ behind, execute a
  (distance)
  180-degree return to the field.

- If the engine fails at 500 feet AGL, select an emergency area that lies within _____ and 90 degrees of turn.
  (distance)

- If the engine fails below 500 feet AGL, select the best area that lies within _____ and 30 degrees of turn.
  (distance)

CHECKLIST: Impending Emergency Landing

- Determine the time you can remain aloft:

  1. Fuel remaining.
  2. Weather conditions.
  3. Daylight left.
  4. Nature of discrepancy.

- Select an adequate airport:

  1. Paved airport is easier to locate.
  2. Repair facilities, emergency facilities.

- Communicate with FSS or ATC.

  1. Call before the situation becomes critical.
  2. Obtain a DF or radar confirmation of your position.
  3. Ask for an updated weather briefing.
  4. Request radar service to the airport.

# 7 | Critical Landing Situations

THERE ARE A NUMBER of landing situations requiring special handling that do not fall into the category of emergency landings — unless the pilot is not prepared to meet the challenge. Let's consider the difficulties that a pilot can expect to encounter when faced with a few of these critical landing situations.

## Mountain Airports

I have seen the wind socks at opposite ends of a mountain runway blowing simultaneously in opposite directions. Obviously, with all those peaks, ridges, and gullies for the wind to flow around, over, and through, tricky crosswinds are a hallmark of a mountain landing. Any pilot planning a flight to the high country would be wise to spend a few windy days resharpening skills at the home airport.

The unexpectedly high touchdown speed brought about by the high-density altitude has caused many flatland pilots to overshoot. Fly your mountain approach at your normal indicated approach speed, naturally. But recognize that your true airspeed is somewhat higher. This, of course, produces a higher ground speed at touchdown, which results in a longer stopping distance. As an example, the touchdown speed at a 4000-foot elevation with the temperature standing at 80°F will be about 10 percent greater than at an airport near sea level. If you would like to see for yourself what this does to the available landing distance, pick a section of your home runway that duplicates the length of the mountain airport. Then practice some landings from an approach speed 10 percent faster than you normally fly. And as you practice your crosswind and "hot landing" techniques, be sure to include some simulated go-arounds, since they are standard practice for the mountain pilot. To make these go-arounds realistic, stack the cards against yourself. First, load your airplane with the weight with which you expect to travel. Second, allow only 75 percent power for the go-around to simulate the power available at a high elevation.

Many mountain airports present another critical landing

situation. They feature a one-way runway. No matter what the wind, you land in a specified direction. This naturally means that you may be called on to execute a "downwind" landing, requiring even more additional ground speed — and another premountain drill at your hometown airport.

## Landing without Brakes

If you don't know the smell of aircraft hydraulic fluid, drop by the maintenance shop for a whiff. Because some day on a downwind leg, that sweet odor in the cockpit may warn you of a brakeless landing.

Landing with defective brakes is not necessarily difficult or dangerous if you are aware of the situation and take positive steps to offset the lack of braking power. You can best make yourself aware of the problem by routinely testing the firmness of the brake pedals while on downwind leg. A soft pedal in an airplane means a leaking brake cylinder and loss of hydraulic fluid, just as it does in an automobile.

Arriving pilots who discover that they are facing a no-brake landing must lay plans to meet the situation. They are particularly interested in three areas of possible difficulty: runway length, crosswind control, and taxiing.

As a general rule, you should select a runway that provides twice the normal required total-to-clear-obstacle landing distance. If the destination airport is not long enough to provide this safety margin, flying to a suitable alternate is in order. Additionally, you should employ your best short-field approach to further ensure an adequate landing distance. And, once down, you should leave the flaps extended for aerodynamic braking. Once the landing roll slows, have a passenger open a cabin door wide against the slipstream to further shorten the roll-out.

Facing a crosswind landing without brakes requires that you know your airplane. You must know from experience the degree that your airplane depends upon brakes for crosswind directional control during the roll-out. If crosswind control depends heavily on brakes and the crosswind is strong, then you would be wise to divert to a runway with a more favorable wind.

Many airplanes have separate brake systems for each main wheel. In these instances it is quite common to lose braking power on one while retaining good brakes on the other. If, on the downwind leg, you have brakes on just one side of your airplane, you may want to change runways to choose the direction of the crosswind you will face on landing and roll-out. You should pick the runway that puts your good brakes downwind from the crosswind. If you have good brakes on only the right wheel, for example, you would rather have the crosswind blowing from the left. It is the brake on the side opposite the crosswind, of course, that prevents the plane from weather-vaning during the roll-out.

Taxiing, the brakeless pilot's final area of concern, can be tricky and dangerous if not well thought out. There are two paramount rules to observe when taxiing without brakes. First, taxi slowly. A "freewheeling" airplane is hard to stop and moments are anxious, as, for example, when you find yourself coasting toward the steel wall of a hangar. I'll not soon forget the day I sat as a passenger in the rear seat of an old Cessna when the brakes went out. The pilot found himself freewheeling toward the churning props of a DC-3 that was warming up its engines. I saw him rear back in his seat to stop the airplane with body English, and right away I began clearing a spot for myself on the floor. The front-seat passenger (a nonpilot, by the way) had the presence of mind to step out of the slow-moving airplane, grab the horizontal stabilizer and hang on. He stopped the airplane with several feet to spare and no damage done, but to this day that pilot ducks noticeably when he taxis near any revving engine.

In addition to taxiing slowly, you should not taxi a brakeless airplane near buildings or other airplanes. When approaching the ramp area, for example, plan to stop your airplane well away from the tiedowns or hangars, and then hand-push the airplane where you want it. If the airplane is on a firm surface that invites easy rolling, you may find that even idle power keeps it moving.

You may need to cut the switches to let the airplane stop.

If you taxi a brakeless airplane, plan ahead. Remember to keep the wind direction in mind. A tail wind, for example, increases taxi speed and makes stopping difficult. When planning a turn that lies ahead, visualize how the wind pushing on the vertical stabilizer will either help or hinder your turning radius.

Be alert for upgrades and downgrades that lie ahead and adjust your taxi power accordingly well in advance of the hill. Try to avoid the necessity of tight turns; if you have brakes on the right wheel, for example, a right 270-degree turn gives you a nice change in direction to the left. Just make sure you plan ahead to allow maneuvering room.

Any pilot would be wise to occasionally practice no-brakes landings. To do this, simply refrain from using brakes as you land, taxi, and bring the airplane to a halt.

## Wake Turbulence

Time was when we small-plane pilots called that disturbed air behind the transports prop wash. That was in the days of the Douglas DC-4s and Lockheed Constellations. The disturbed currents in the wake of the airliners made our landings difficult, and that difficulty seemed to come from those big four-bladed propellers. Then the Jet Liners came along, and the airlines retired the prop-driven airplanes. Yet the prop wash didn't disappear from the runways we shared with the likes of Boeing 707s, DC-8s, and later, 747s. In fact that prop wash seemed to get progressively more potent as the propellerless Jet Liners got bigger and bigger.

And so we learned the true nature of wake turbulence — wing-tip vortex. This vortex is a horizontal whirlwind that slides off each wing tip any time the wing is producing lift. The heavier the airplane, the greater the lift and the stronger the vortex.

The rotational velocity of a vortex immediately behind a heavy jet's wing tip can easily exceed 100 knots. As bad as this windstorm sounds, it rarely inflicts in-flight structural damage on small airplanes that fly into the jet's wake turbulence. Light-plane pilots who let themselves get caught up in the vortices, however, can expect to lose control of their airplanes momentarily. This loss of control results from the rolling movement of the vortex that exceeds the small airplane's rate of roll. The pilot in this case just doesn't have a rolling capability with which to counter the vortex roll. If this loss of control occurs at pattern altitude or below, it is certainly possible for the airplane to fly into an obstruction or the ground, and then structural damage *will* occur.

Wake turbulence from large aircraft holds the potential for damage and injury. Accordingly, the small-plane pilot should consider any landing that shares the pattern with large planes as a critical landing situation. You must plan your approach and landing to avoid an encounter with wake turbulence.

The first step in avoiding wake turbulence is to understand its behavior. Once you know the characteristics of wing-tip vortices, you can visualize the wake's location and easily plan your landing to avoid it. Wing-tip vortices exhibit four basic characteristics:

1. Vortices are produced only when the wings are producing lift.
2. Vortices settle downward and fan out laterally left and right.
3. Vortices drift with the wind.
4. Vortex strength weakens with time and distance.

Let's look at a few common landing situations and apply some vortex avoidance procedures to them.

LANDING ON THE SAME RUNWAY BEHIND A HEAVY AIRCRAFT. If practical, separate your landing from the heavy airplane's touchdown with adequate time or distance. As a rule of thumb, 3 minutes or 4 miles separation on final approach should allow the wake turbulence to dissipate. If this degree of separation is impractical, plan an approach path slightly above that flown by the heavy airplane. This avoids the settling vortices. Then note the heavy airplane's touchdown point and plan to land beyond it. Once the wings quit providing lift, the vortex action soon ceases.

**LANDING ON A PARALLEL RUNWAY BEHIND A HEAVY AIRPLANE.** Again, adequate separation behind the landing airplane is the best defense against encountering wake turbulence. If you do not have ample separation on final approach, be alert for the wake turbulence that may drift over to your final approach path and runway. Stay above the heavy airplane's flight path and land well beyond its touchdown point.

**LANDING AFTER A HEAVY AIRPLANE HAS LANDED ON AN INTER-SECTING RUNWAY.** If possible, land to hold short of the intersection. If unable to do this and the runway is long, cross the intersection above the heavy airplane's path and land well beyond the intersection.

**LANDING BEHIND A DEPARTING HEAVY AIRPLANE ON THE SAME OR PARALLEL RUNWAY.** Note the heavy airplane's point of rotation (where vortex action begins) and land prior to reaching that point.

**LANDING BEHIND A HEAVY AIRPLANE THAT IS DEPARTING FROM A CROSSING RUNWAY.** Plan to land short of the crossing runway. Even if the heavy airplane's rotation point lies beyond the intersection, the engine's takeoff power produces a jet blast that can upset your landing.

## Jet Blast

The engine exhaust from jet airplanes can be a serious threat to light airplanes. Here are some rules of thumb for minimum separation to help you avoid jet blast velocities in excess of 30 knots:

|  | Idle power | Breakaway power | Takeoff power |
|---|---|---|---|
| Corporate-size jets | 100 feet | 200 feet | 400 feet |
| Midsize jets | 150 feet | 300 feet | 600 feet |
| Heavy jets | 300 feet | 600 feet | 1500 feet |

# IN REVIEW: Critical Landing Situations

- Any pilot planning a flight to a mountain airport should review short-field crosswind landing techniques.
- A "soft" pedal or whiff of hydraulic fluid on the downwind leg may warn of a brakeless landing.
- A no-brakes landing presents three areas of possible difficulty:
  1. Runway length.
  2. Crosswind control.
  3. Taxiing.
- Allow an extra margin of runway length when landing with defective brakes and use your short-field landing procedures.
- If your airplane relies heavily on brakes for crosswind control during roll-out, you may want to divert to a more favorable runway.
- When taxiing with defective brakes, follow three rules:
  1. Taxi slowly.
  2. Do not taxi near other airplanes or buildings.
  3. Plan ahead to evaluate wind effect, allow maneuvering room, and compensate for any downhill or uphill grade.
- Knowing the characterics of wing-tip vortices allows a pilot to visualize the location of wake turbulence:
  1. Vortices are produced any time the wings produce lift.
  2. Vortices settle downward and fan out laterally.
  3. Vortices drift with the wind.
  4. Vortex strength weakens with time and distance.

# 8 | Slip to a Landing

WHEN GRIZZLED OLD PILOTS sit in the lobby of a modern airport, they tend to hunch in the far corner of the room and mumble about how the slip to a landing has become "the lost art of flying." And of course they are right. After all, what good is a slip nowadays? In the old days it was a pilot's only means to steepen an approach over the treetops and onto the short landing strip. But now we have efficient flaps and longer runways. Therefore the slip to a landing has become an outmoded, inefficient, and unsophisticated means to steepen an approach. But it also, by the way, provides some of the greatest fun that flying has to offer.

Pilots who can skillfully slip their airplanes seem to get no end of pleasure from the procedure – stiffening the slip to increase the rate of sink, reducing the sink at will with a deft flick of aileron and rudder, steepening the glide path a final time with a mash of rudder, landing the airplane exactly where they want it. The difference between accuracy landing and just getting it down is whether or not they plant the airplane's upwind wheel exactly dead center on a hubcap-sized touchdown target.

Probably the best first step in learning the slip is to simply stand near the runway's end and watch a bunch of airplanes slip in over the tree line, studying the maneuver from a vantage point outside the cockpit. You won't find these slips going on at a big city airport catering to Bonanzas, Mooneys, King Airs, and the like. Instead, go out to the uncontrolled sod field that fills its pattern with Luscombes, Cubs, and Taylorcrafts. Study each little ship as its pilot slips to a butterfly touchdown on the turf. And, make no mistake, those planes don't really need to slip. They could easily make two or three landings on the average country runway of today. They do a slip just because it's fun and looks good.

The purpose of a slip to a landing is merely to steepen the glide path on final approach without increasing the airplane's airspeed. Pilots accomplish this feat by simply flying the airplane sidewise through the air.

To see how this maneuver works, imagine a pilot who has just turned from base leg and is now established on final approach. At this point, the pilot realizes that the approach is too high and decides to steepen it with a slip.

The first move is simple — close the throttle to idle power. It would make little sense to lose altitude with a slip while maintaining power that tends to reduce the sink rate.

Once the throttle is closed, the next step is to determine the direction of the crosswind blowing over the runway. True, the direction of the crosswind has little effect on the slip during the approach. But somewhere prior to touchdown, the pilot must shift from the "slip to a landing" to the "slip for the crosswind correction." And this shift is easier to accomplish if the pilot has slipped with the "down-wing" into the wind.

Assuming that the pilot is facing a left crosswind on landing, the slip is established by using considerable aileron to bank left while simultaneously mashing in firm right rudder to swing the airplane's fuselage to the right and at an angle to the forward flight path. With equally firm aileron and rudder pressures, the airplane descends straight ahead but flies sidewise through the air — banked left, yawed right.

It is this sidewise flight attitude that steepens the approach. The attitude presents the side of the fuselage to the oncoming relative wind. The excess drag that the maneuver creates causes the airplane's descent to steepen appreciably. And yet the steepness of the approach is easy to control. If the pilot wishes to steepen the approach even further, additional aileron and rudder pressure is applied. The extra rudder swings even more fuselage into the wind, while extra aileron keeps the descent going straight ahead. Conversely, if the pilot wishes to lessen the airplane's rate of sink, the control pressures are decreased. This reduces the fuselage's sidewise attitude and lessens the drag. The pilot can then control the rate of descent to make a perfect glide path toward the touchdown target.

But here is the tricky part — the pilot must maintain the

proper approach speed throughout the slip to a landing. And that requires knowledge of the airplane, since in many airplanes the airspeed indicator is inaccurate during the slip. This inaccuracy stems from a pitot tube that is not aligned with the wind and a static port that may no longer be receiving neutral pressure as the fuselage is turned into the wind. And add to this fact that the airspeed changes during the cross-controlled attitude. Many airplanes slow down with the extra drag of the slip, and the pilot must lower the nose slightly to maintain flying speed. Some airplanes, on the other hand, may tend to gain speed in the slip. In either case, the pilot must know the airplane well enough to determine the correct airspeed by the sound of the wind over the windshield and the feel of the controls. As the pilot rolls out of the slip, the airplane's nose must be returned quickly to the attitude that will continue to produce the correct approach speed.

Once the pilot has brought the airplane down accurately toward the touchdown target, there is a shift from the "slip to a landing" to the "crosswind correction slip." To do this, simply release enough rudder pressure to let the fuselage align with the flight path and the runway centerline, maintaining enough aileron, of course, to correct for the crosswind (as described in Chapter 2).

Pilots sometimes ask what the difference is between a slip used to correct a crosswind and a slip used to lose altitude. The only difference lies in the degree of the slip, the degree of control pressures. In a slip used to correct for a crosswind only enough aileron is used to prevent the airplane from drifting, and only enough rudder is applied to keep the fuselage aligned with the flight path. In correcting for a left wind, for example, the airplane is banked to the left, but the nose points straight ahead. In a slip used to lose altutide, however, strong rudder pressure is applied to deflect the fuselage away from the flight path, while considerable opposite aileron keeps the airplane's flight path on course. The airplane's wings are banked left while the airplane's nose is deflected to the right, for example.

Begin your in-flight practice by taking your airplane to 3000 feet. First, of course, review your airplane's flight manual to make certain that prolonged slips are an approved maneuver; a few models prohibit them. At this altitude, align your airplane with a road and throttle back, leaving 1500 RPM in the engine to keep it warm. Then practice rolling into and out of the slip as you descend a few hundred feet.

After you feel comfortable with the cross-control attitude of the slip, carry your practice to a runway for the full approach and landing sequence. Practice until you are good — really good. Then carry your act to an audience that will appreciate your skill, a country airport pattern. And spend the afternoon in the company of those Cubs, Luscombes, and Taylorcrafts as you help to preserve "the lost art of flying."

## IN REVIEW: Slip to a Landing

- The purpose of a slip to a landing is to steepen the glide path on final approach without increasing the airplane's airspeed.
- The maneuver is accomplished by flying the airplane sidewise.
- Begin the slip by first closing the throttle.
- Slip with the "down-wing" toward the direction of any crosswind.
- Establish the slip by using considerable aileron to bank the wings into the wind while simultaneously applying firm rudder to yaw the fuselage in the opposite direction.
- The excess drag that the yawed fuselage creates causes the airplane's descent to steepen.
- If you wish to further steepen your approach, you must apply additional rudder and aileron pressures.
- If you wish to lessen the airplane's rate of sink, you must reduce the control pressures.
- During a slip the airspeed indicator may be inaccurate.
- You must determine your airspeed by the sound of the slipstream and the feel of the controls.

- Adjust the pitch attitude to maintain the correct approach speed throughout the maneuver.
- Practice your slips at altitude before you begin slipping to a landing.

# 9 | Landing Tailwheel Airplanes

THERE'S SOMETHING ABOUT a tailwheel airplane that lets mere *aviation* become *flying*. Even the gently rocking taxi, as you lean back against the tailwheel, holds promise of adventure. That extra move on the takeoff run — as the tail steps up for liftoff — puts the bush pilot twang into any flight. And once aloft, they stay tailwheelers because most tailwheel airplanes tend to be rather antiquated noisy affairs made up of drag-producing struts, cramped cockpits that reek of hot oil, and taut fabric that lets your fingertips feel the engine's pulse. Some let you hold that clattering engine in your lap; others hand you a long wooden stick with which to guide ailerons and elevator; a few even let you open the cockpit's Plexiglas shelter to listen for the wind-in-the-struts song of flying, let you lean into the slipstream for a face-flattening cyclone of prop blast, let you hear firsthand, behind the throttled engine, the whispered return to Earth.

No matter how long you've been at flying, there is something about a tailwheeler that recalls the legacy: magnificent men and flying machines, canvas-armored Sopwiths, barnstormers, the night mail, and now you, behind the controls of this noisy throwback of an airplane.

For the pilot willing to take them on, tailwheelers offer a splendid bonus — a physical contact with history's golden age of flying. And, let me say this right off, landing a tailwheeler is no more difficult than landing an airplane with a nosewheel. It's just different, that's all. But let me also say that the difference is great enough that you cannot expect to teach yourself tailwheel landings. A good flight instructor is called for. An incident I witnessed a few years ago points up this need.

I had just landed at a neighboring airport and taxied past the Fixed Base Operator (FBO) to the maintenance hangar. The field had once served the navy, and the hangar was one of those cavernous metal buildings with mammoth doors that could swallow two zeppelins.

It was a slow summer day and several mechanics and linemen stood talking just inside the hangar, taking advantage of the cooling breeze and protecting shade. Outside, across the sunny concrete ramp, the new owner of an old tailwheeler was polishing the windshield. The pretty little ship was a prewar model, painted pale yellow with cream trim, and it stood high on stiff Luscombe legs, facing us. The owner was waiting on his instructor for his first checkout ride in the airplane. Hoping to save the instructor a long hot walk from the FBO (so he later said), he called a lineman over to spin the propeller for him. Surely, he felt, he could at least taxi the 100 yards to the airport office.

The "contact" was given and acknowledged, the lineman spun the prop, and the little 65 cranked and idled with a *topoptika, topoptika* barely heard by us in the open hangar. Then the pilot added taxi power to pull ahead. When he started to turn, the airplane started to swerve. Now, correcting a minor swerve in a tailwheel airplane presents little difficulty, unless you are attempting to do so by the learn-while-you-swerve method.

The lineman knew the pilot was tailwheel inexperienced, saw that he was not correcting for the swerve, and immediately feared for the airplanes that were tied down nearby. So he made a running leap and grabbed a strut on the outside wing to stop the action. The action didn't stop. In fact, the swerve grew into a series of lazy circles, with the lineman hanging on and "riding the whip," skater fashion. The airplane made three 360s before the dazed lineman turned loose. (Later, as we were putting it all together, we recalled smoke coming from the lineman's skidding shoes.)

When the lineman dropped away, the airplane did momentarily straighten out — directly toward the open hangar. Milling about in the doorway, we were of divided minds. Some made a dash *toward* the fight, while the rest of us dodged *away* from the approaching juggernaut. When the airplane entered the hangar, reverberating echos made the soft chugging of the taxiing engine sound like something off the wing of a B-29. There was a lot of arm waving and shouted instructions to the pilot, but as he whizzed past, the glazed look in his eyes told me he had lost interest in the whole affair.

The airplane caromed off the tail section of a Cherokee, whacked the shop's pickup with a wing, and threw itself nose first into the hangar's far rear corner. There, among the clatter and clamor of splintering wood and delicate duralumin tearing against steel hangar wall, the little yellow ship fitfully beat itself to pieces.

Well, damage was substantial, but miraculously no one was hurt (although I understand the pilot was never again quite himself).

The point of the whole story, of course, is that we cannot safely teach ourselves how to handle a tailwheel airplane. An instructor is needed from the first "contact."

Carefully choose your instructor, who should be thoroughly familiar with the model you intend to check out. Because in order to let you learn firsthand the landing capabilities of your airplane, you must be permitted to go right to the machine's limits. And this means that you occasionally test your instructor's ability to make a recovery. Your instructor must know that airplane!

And, if at all possible, select an instructor with a good sense of humor. Chances are you will do some genuinely funny things as you master the airplane. Things, for example, like working the elevator exactly out of phase with the bunny-hops as you attempt to correct your first bounced landing. (Instructor says: "I got it! I got it!") Or the first landing you make with a foot on one brake. (Instructor says: "Well, at least you know which way it's gonna ground loop.") Having an instructor with a sense of humor aboard lets you share the mirth.

But before you choose your instructor and start the check-out, let's pinpoint the one great difference between nosewheel and tailwheel airplanes. This difference gives the tailwheel airplane its landing characteristics, and simply put, it is that the main gear of a nosewheel airplane lies *behind* the center of gravity, whereas on a tailwheel airplane, it lies *ahead* of the center of gravity. It is necessary that the landing gears be so arranged, because a nosewheel airplane with its weight behind the main gear would rest with its tail on the ground, and the tailwheel with its weight forward would rest with its nose on the ground (Figs. 9.1, 9.2).

**Fig. 9.1.** The one great difference between nosewheelers and tailwheelers is simply this: the main gear of a nosewheeler lies behind the center of gravity, and on a tailwheeler the gear is ahead of the center of gravity.

**Fig. 9.2.** A nosewheel airplane with a center of gravity aft of the main gear would rest with its tail on the ground. A center of gravity ahead of a taildragger's gear would put the airplane's nose to the ground.

A tailwheel pilot must understand the significance of a center of gravity that lies behind the landing gear. Once you understand the significance, you know what to expect when landing your tailwheeler. To understand the forces at work, let's visualize "center of gravity." Rather than think of it as the designer's small cross on a drawing that denotes the center of mass, let's picture it in our minds as a great, black, iron cannonball. Load this cannonball in the fuselage ahead of the main gear of a nosewheel airplane and behind the gear of a tailwheeler. Then let's set each airplane rolling down the runway with its cannonball aboard. Now, which airplane has the greater tendency to turn end-around? The tailwheeler, naturally, with its center of gravity behind the wheels. Each small swerve gives that cannonball momentum; the tail tries to overtake the nose. On the other hand, the nosewheeler's center of gravity, located in front of the wheels, actually tends to straighten out any swerve (Fig. 9.3).

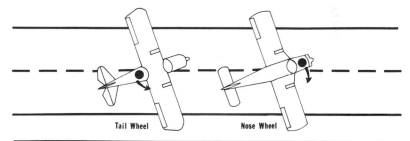

**Fig. 9.3** The big difference between tailwheelers and nosewheelers is this: A center of gravity that lies ahead of the main wheels tends to stabilize ground handling.

In landing a tailwheel airplane, then, you have an important task to perform, one which is not nearly so vital in a nosewheeler. You must try to land with a degree of perfection that prevents a swerve from ever starting; if a swerve should start, you must prevent it from gaining momentum.

Let's see how a tailwheeler's center of gravity invites a swerve and how the nosewheel design minimizes a swerve during several stages of the landing.

## Touchdown

It is important that a tailwheel airplane touch down with a perfect crosswind correction and at a precise landing speed. Visualize the cannonball behind the landing gear. If the tail-wheeler touches down in a crab angle or while drifting, the momentum starts to swing the ball. The same thing happens with a tricycle-gear airplane, of course, but with a slight difference. Here, if the airplane touches in a crab, the center of gravity ahead of the wheels tends to bring the nose around straight, and once the nose wheel contacts the runway, it tends to act as a brace against the drifting airplane.

Proper touchdown speed is critical to a smooth landing in a tailwheeler. The airplane must dissipate its flying speed before it lands; it must touch down "full-stall." This speed actually translates to the "three point attitude" (all three tires touch at once), which is also, of course, the stall attitude of the airplane. Two undesirable things take place if the tailwheeler touches tail high with flying speed remaining. First, the momentum of the touchdown sends the cannonball (and the tail) hurtling downward. This in turn increases the wing's angle of attack, and with a smidge of flying speed remaining, the airplane lifts off.

Late in your tailwheel checkout the instructor will probably have you doing "wheel landings." Here you literally fly the airplane onto the runway and touch down with a few miles of flying speed remaining and the tailwheel far above the runway. But you will also be taught a method of preventing the touchdown's momentum from forcing the tail downward to produce an increase in the wing's angle of attack. You probably will be asked to exert forward stick pressure as the tires touch, to keep the tail high and prevent an unwanted liftoff.

Since the touchdown attitude (and the resultant touchdown

speed) is so important to a tailwheel landing, here is a suggestion: Before you start your formal checkout, ride as a passenger in the airplane. Have your pilot taxi you around so that the three-point landing attitude is familiar to you. Then ask your instructor to fast-taxi down the runway with the tailwheel several inches above the ground; this is the "wheel landing" attitude. Finally, take an outside look at the three-point attitude. Notice how the ship rests in contact with the ground on the backside of the tires. Carry that mental image as you land your airplane.

## Roll-Out

During the roll-out, some of your control over that loose cannonball behind the cockpit is taken from you, since much of the rudder control disappears as you slow down. The "steerable tailwheel" is marginally steerable, and the brakes on most taildraggers were obviously designed by a demolition-derby driver who had no intention of stopping anyway. Modern tricycle-gear airplanes, on the other hand, provide good nosewheel steering and disk brakes.

So during the tailwheeler roll-out, make the best use of the control that remains. You may not be able to prevent small swerves from occurring, but alertness and quick action easily keep them under control. Alertness in this case means keeping your eyes straight ahead and remaining aware of how your airplane's fuselage is lined up with the centerline. If you look inside the cockpit to reach for a knob or switch — even momentarily — a significant swerve is likely. If your runway has no centerline, focus your attention on the far end of the runway during the roll-out. This gives you a reasonably good straight-line reference.

Quick action to minimize the swerves during roll-out means anticipating the correction so that control pressures are given the instant they are needed. This ability to anticipate is not really hard to learn. It's just developing a feel for the direction that the swerve is about to take, and it can be related to some childhood games. Did you ever balance on a rail, standing with one foot behind the other? You soon learned to "feel" which way you were about to tip and simply applied body English to prevent it. Where did you "feel" the balance? In your seat. Remember the "slow race" on your bicycle? Who could ride the slowest without falling? Again, the feel in the seat of your pants told you which way to weave the handlebar. The same goes with anticipating your airplane's swerve. Concentration and the seat of your pants give positive control.

## Taxiing to the Ramp

A normal breeze passes almost unnoticed when you taxi a tricycle plane; the nosewheel acts as a sea anchor when a puff of wind hits the vertical stabilizer. But a tailwheeler often wants to weather-vane like a wind sock. The secret here is undiminished vigilance. Plan ahead so that if an upcoming turn places the force of the wind against your vertical stabilizer, you can slow your airplane and decide if the direction of the wind force calls for more or less turning on your part.

Quartering winds as you taxi are more noticeable without the stabilizing effect of a nosewheel. Proper stick control has the elevator deflected up in a quartering head wind and down when the wind is from the rear. Both moves, of course, are designed to keep the wind away from the bottom surface of the elevator. A quartering head wind calls for up aileron in the direction of the wind, whereas a tailing wind requires down aileron held against it.

For more fun if you are very lucky, you may be too short to see directly over the nose as you taxi. Then you will have to S-turn as did those pilots of old in their long-legged and high-tired biplanes. S-turns ask you to weave left and stretch your neck right, then weave right and stretch left, all the way to the ramp. S-turning takes a lot of taxiway. And if you meet a modern tricycle-gear airplane taxiing toward you, don't expect him to recognize your plight. Just pull over to the side and stop to let him and his sleek-swept tail, purring engine, and streamlined wings scoot past.

There you have it. All that's left now is to rent a taildragger, choose an instructor, load your great black cannonball aboard, and go back to touch flying's golden age (Fig. 9.4).

**Fig. 9.4.** It is very difficult for a pilot to land a taildragger and *not* recall the legacy.

## IN REVIEW: Tailwheel Landings

- The one great difference between nosewheel and tailwheel airplanes is the position of the center of gravity.
- The main gear of a nosewheel airplane lies *behind* the center of gravity, and, on a tailwheeler, lies *ahead* of the center of gravity.
- A center of gravity that lies ahead of the main wheels tends to stabilize the roll-out.

# 10 | Cardinal Rules for Perfect Landings

NOWADAYS, we seem to like our information in capsule form. With this in mind, I'd like to list the 10 rules that I feel are paramount in landing an airplane.

Know both the landing capability of your airplane, and your own ability to employ that capability. Do not count on either yourself or your airplane to perform beyond these demonstrated abilities. The aircraft handbook's landing charts provide a guide for determining the aircraft's capability. Your piloting skill, however, can be determined only by observing and evaluating your performance with every landing. Expend the effort to discover the performance that you and your airplane as a team can deliver in terms of accuracy, smoothness, crosswind correction, and landing distance.

Carefully evaluate the landing conditions anytime reason tells you that they will test the capabilities of you or your airplane. All too often a landing accident occurs simply because a pilot thinks to himself, "That's an approved runway down there, and I'm flying an approved airplane. The landing will work out OK." Cold logic tells us that this is not necessarily true; runways and airplanes offer no guarantees.

Even the destination runway that has accepted your airplane many times in the past can hold new surprises. Picture yourself arriving at that grass field you've previously enjoyed. But today as you turn downwind, you see that the grass surface is wet and slick from a brief shower. The sock is half-filled and swinging square with the runway. And a sailplane crew readying their ship at the approach end of the strip forces your touchdown point another 100 yards down the runway. Suddenly the familiar airport presents a challenge. You must carefully evaluate all the factors against the airplane's landing performance charts and your own skill.

③

Plan your approach to the traffic pattern. A good landing begins with a proper approach to the pattern. It has been my observation that an improper pattern entry places unnecessary stress on pilots as they find themselves in the wrong places and maneuvering sharply to put things right.

To assure a correct approach, know both the active runway and the leg you intend to enter well before you reach the airport. Then fly to a landmark a few miles from the pattern to allow a correct entry heading and altitude.

④

Fly an accurate pattern. A good pattern is designed to give you time to ready your airplane for the landing and to plan an orderly final approach while keeping the action close to the airport. To make it work, fly an accurate altitude and ground track at an appropriate airspeed. All this means flying with precision, knowing how the wind affects time and drift on each leg, and selecting landmarks to define the desired ground track.

⑤

Make your go-around decision before you start descending on final approach. Most landing accidents could have been avoided if the pilot had made a go-around. In many of these cases, the pilots failed to make a go-around simply because they hadn't made plans for its use until the pressing need was suddenly at hand. Then, when preoccupied with the critical situation and aircraft control, they simply did not think to go around. Prevent this from happening to you; select a go-around point on the runway while still on downwind. And make the decision then to go around if all things are not going well by the time you reach that point.

Make every landing an accuracy landing. As you accumulate hours aloft, your landing skill will get either better or worse; it certainly will not remain unchanged. And those hundreds of practiced accuracy landings will be invaluable when you suddenly face a situation that demands accuracy. An accurate landing depends heavily on a good glide path, precise airspeed control, and a touchdown target on the runway.

Do not perform any "clean-up" procedures until you clear the runway and bring the airplane to a halt. If you look down to close the carburetor heat, raise the flaps, or tune the radio while the airplane is rolling, you are in danger of hitting something or, at the very least, scaring your passengers with a swerve.

Maintain your crosswind skill. This skill is one very likely to get rusty, and the best way to keep it up to par is through periodic dual sessions. Remember, nearly all landing accidents result from the pilot's inability to handle the crosswind.

⑨

Fly with a contingency plan for an emergency landing in mind. It is very difficult to come up with a plan from scratch when the engine starts sputtering. I do not mean to imply that under ordinary circumstances a pilot needs to have a landing site in view at all times. Today's airplanes and engines are a bit more reliable than that, and a malfunction rarely knocks down an airplane immediately. But a pilot should have a nearby alternate airport in mind at all times as well as the heading and the time that will take him there. Once a malfunction, serious weather, rough terrain, or low fuel does present itself, however, the pilot is no longer flying under ordinary circumstances. At this point, he will attempt to keep a landing site in view at all times.

# 10

Exert a 100 percent effort in every landing. Remember, even the pros must put forth a maximum effort to achieve perfect landings. A maximum effort here means that you have learned the capabilities of your airplane, know the factors that influence landings, and use your skill to control those factors. You have, in fact, a total awareness of your airplane, the environment, and yourself. Make a commitment to that degree of effort and you cannot fail to deliver perfect landing after perfect landing.

# INDEX